Temptation

Other Books by Wayne E. Oates

Behind the Masks:
Personality Disorders in Religious Behavior

The Struggle to Be Free:
My Story and Your Story

The Christian Pastor
Third Edition, Revised

Your Particular Grief

The Religious Care of the Psychiatric Patient

Pastoral Counseling

POTENTIALS: GUIDES FOR PRODUCTIVE LIVING
Books 1–11, edited by Wayne E. Oates

Convictions That Give You Confidence

Your Right to Rest

CHRISTIAN CARE BOOKS
Books 1–12, edited by Wayne E. Oates

Pastor's Handbook, Vols. I and II

WITH CHARLES E. OATES

People in Pain: Guidelines for Pastoral Care

Temptation

A Biblical and Psychological Approach

Wayne E. Oates

Westminster/John Knox Press
Louisville, Kentucky

Book design by Ken Taylor

First edition

Published by Westminster/John Knox Press
Louisville, Kentucky

PRINTED IN THE UNITED STATES OF AMERICA
9 8 7 6 5 4 3 2 1

Library of Congress Cataloging-in-Publication Data

Oates, Wayne Edward, 1917–
    Temptation : a Biblical and psychological approach / Wayne E. Oates. — 1st ed.
        p.   cm.
    Includes bibliographical references.
    ISBN 0-664-25113-7
    1. Temptation.   2. Temptation—Psychological aspects.   I. Title.
BT725.038   1991
241'.3—dc20   90-22813

In memoriam

LESLIE VAN NOSTRAND, M.D.

Contents

Acknowledgments

I celebrate, with the publication of this book, my fortieth year with The Westminster Press. Since our last book, *Beyond the Masks: Personality Disorders in Religious Behavior* (1987), The Westminster Press has merged with John Knox Press to become Westminster/John Knox. In doing so the presses have moved from Philadelphia and Atlanta, respectively, to my own home city of Louisville, Kentucky. I am elated to have them so near that I can call them on the local exchange or, better, visit in their offices or over lunch to do our work. I am especially indebted to Alexa Smith and Harold Twiss for the thoughtful and creative editorial suggestions they have made.

Furthermore, I appreciate the work of my colleagues James Hyde and Henlee Barnette, especially their scholarly fellowship as we have conversed about the ideas presented in this book. Their comradeship, woven as it is into the fabric of our daily care of intensely upset and lonely people, is a here-and-now expression of the kingdom of Heaven.

I want to thank Donna Lynch Raley and Pam Metté for their professional skill and personal patience in preparing the manuscript in its original and revised forms.

My wife, Pauline Rhodes Oates, has been my confidante and inspiration, providing tranquillity and steadfastness to me. She has, through the mystique of her being, been an unfailing source of energy and wisdom for this work of ministry.

W.E.O.

PROLOGUE

Whatever
Became of Temptation?

When was the last time you heard a sermon, read an article or a book, or had a serious conversation with a friend about temptation? The word is still in our dictionaries, but it is not used very much. We can rightly ask, "Whatever became of temptation?"

As I began gathering materials for writing this book, I was immediately struck by the scarcity of contemporary books and serious articles on temptation. I discussed this with a colleague of mine, Douglas P. Hobson, M.D., a psychiatrist with the U.S. Diplomatic Corps. In a letter to me he wrote, "Perhaps the absence of material on temptation reflects the permissive and promiscuous society in which we live, where there are fewer temptations because there are fewer sins, or at least less talk about sin."

Karl Menninger, in his book *Whatever Became of Sin?*, notes that legal and medical interpretations of human behavior have replaced pastoral and theological interpretations. He writes (p. 51), "There ought to be a law, says someone, and, before long, the law has been enacted and an old 'sin' has become a new crime. This is where many sins have gone." In the process, the temptation goes with the sin. Human behavior then becomes a matter of not getting caught breaking the law. The searching of our consciences in the struggle with temptation—for which we are responsible to God as well as to neighbor and self—is replaced by the assumption that if an act is legal we need not worry about whether it is unethical.

Menninger goes further and says that many activities formerly considered to be sins have now come to be seen as symptoms of disorder or disease. "Some behavior once called 'crime' has been relabeled 'illness.' Some sins which never have been proscribed by law and labeled as crimes are also regarded now as symptomatic" (p. 93). When we ask whatever became of temptation, Menninger's and Hobson's observations about sin are pertinent to our loss of consciousness and conscience about temptation.

Is It a Sin to Be Tempted?

However, our quest for whatever happened to temptation must be pushed further. Religious communities themselves seem to have neglected the realm of temptation. Among religious groups, temptation is almost a taboo subject. "To be tempted is to sin" is the conventional religious assumption. To think about or feel impelled to move in a certain forbidden direction is interpreted as being "as bad" as actually doing it. This interpretation grows out of a misinterpretation of scripture. We are told in the Bible that Jesus "in every respect has been tempted as we are, yet [is] without sin" (Heb. 4:15). Temptation and sin are distinctly separate from each other in the life of Jesus.

Another misinterpretation of scripture reinforces the assumption that to be tempted is a sin. It is found in explanations of the words of Jesus in the Sermon on the Mount that having hatred or lust within our thoughts is having already committed murder or adultery in our hearts (see Matt. 5:21–30). To the contrary, it seems to me that Jesus is deliberately removing the issues of anger and lust from the public courts of the scribes and Pharisees to the internal forum where God—"unto whom all hearts are open, all desires known, and from whom no secrets are hid" (*Book of Common Prayer*, p. 67)—sifts and puts to the test the very motives of our hearts that lead to sin. God is at the heart of our desire, whether we respond negatively or positively to God's presence. "Then desire," as James 1:15 says, "when it has conceived gives birth to sin; and sin when it is full-grown brings forth death." Even so, God contends with us in our sin.

This process takes place in the internal forum. The internal forum is the arena of temptation, where behavior is debated, scrutinized, and assessed before God in the same way Jesus wrestled with temptation in the wilderness. Common sense would teach a person with gumption that the thought of rage or lust is not the same or as bad as the act, especially to the victim. Temptation is where the process of preventing sin occurs. God is present in this internal forum.

Ecclesiastical Neglect of Temptation

Another answer to the question "Whatever became of temptation?" can be found in the deletion of temptation from the message of the churches and the leadership of their people. To put it more bluntly, people are moved more easily to join the church if they are made to feel guilty. If, without an evangelistic hard sell, they are offered understanding and fellowship as they pour out the story of their struggles with temptation, of their hindrances to prayer, and of their low self-worth before God and in relation to others, they may or may not join the church. This is especially true if there is no heavy-handed sales pitch.

Consequently, the churches themselves have in too many instances sacrificed individualized, personal participation with people in their temptations. Instead, they have increased the size of their congregations, budgets, and buildings on a mass-produced basis. Inner temptations are ignored. The message becomes a shrunken version of the whole counsel of God, our God who in Jesus Christ endured temptation and encourages us "with confidence [to] draw near to the throne of grace, that we may receive mercy and find grace to help in time of need" (Heb. 4:16).

The Reappearance of Temptation

Religious persons may ask, "Whatever became of temptation?" Our lack of awareness of temptation does not mean it has vanished. It has gone somewhere else. It has reappeared in the realm of psychotherapy. Whereas pastors do not usually have time to struggle with individuals in the inmost testings of their spirits, psychotherapists do this day in and day out. People are willing to pay, to "purchase friendship," in order to sort out their emotions and find guidance. Neither they nor their therapists call these emotions "temptations." Rage, fear, bondage, shame, guilt, worthlessness, and many others—which are abundant in the psalms and in the letters of Paul especially—are labeled with psychological terms. The main difference is that in psychotherapy these emotions are not ordinarily lived out in the consciousness of the presence of God. However, individual psychotherapists in increasing numbers are beginning to relate work with clients to their experience of God's presence.

A second difference is that the psychotherapeutic process is carried out in a language system unrelated to the language of scripture, which is also the language of much great literature and the language in which uneducated people ordinarily speak. Psychological language is that of the elite; biblical language is more available to the masses. Psychological language is spoken by educated, privileged persons who are able to afford the friendship offered by psychotherapists. How ironic that, while underprivileged people's speech is saturated with the Elizabethan idiom of Shakespeare and the King James Version of the Bible, these have been replaced in the speech of the educated and privileged by psychological and psychiatric jargon! Nevertheless, the essential content and process of the biblical understanding of temptation has reappeared in the psychotherapeutic relationship. This reappearance stimulated the writing of this book.

Some Purposes of This Book

The primary purpose of this book is to demonstrate the function of temptation in the formation of character. Temptation is the crucible of human character formation. In the most basic way, my hope is to portray how Christian character is put to the test in the decision making that temptation involves. The apostle Paul expressed my prayer in writing this book when he said, "I am again in travail until Christ be formed in you!" (Gal. 4:19). Character formation spans a lifetime. It is a never-ending process. God created each of us to go through times of change, from birth to death. At each developmental crisis, God puts us to the test: will we move forward in growth, fixate where we are, or regress out of fear and loss of the courage to become what Christ would have us become? At each crisis God as Creator tests us. Christ as fellow sufferer accompanies us.

A second purpose is to seek to develop a holistic perception of the biblical and psychological perspectives of temptation. Long before the emergence of psychology as an empirical science, the psychology and the theology of temptation were dealt with in a unified manner by Augustine (354–430) in his *Confessions,* by Martin Luther (1483–1546) in his commentaries on the scriptures, by John Milton (1608–1674) in *Paradise Lost,* and by many others.

Even in this century T. S. Eliot, in *Murder in the Cathedral,* and Archibald MacLeish, in his play *J.B.,* describe vividly the struggle to maintain integrity in the face of temptation and tempters. These authors had no need to integrate psychology and theology. They "saw life steadily and saw it whole," as did

Matthew Arnold's friend. They presented humankind under temptation in a unified, integrated way. They did not invent new vocabularies to make the truth about human temptation into a professional in-group way of speaking. Their grasp of the human situation of temptation was steadfast, precise, and thorough. One of my hopes is to make this wisdom evident here.

A third purpose of this book is to present an appreciation of the spirituality that is quietly present in the work of psychotherapists in their perceptions of temptation. More and more churches and theologians are shutting down their ordered attention to temptation and becoming concerned only with sin and salvation. Meanwhile, the larger community outside the churches has been increasingly concerned with inner motives, the conflictual internal forum of temptation and decision making. These so-called "secular" people are at work outside the tidy confines of pietism. They belong to the *"saeculum,"* the people of this age and time; they are of "this world." Yet without even knowing it, they may be closer to the kingdom of God than the religionists who cannot speak to themselves or others of their temptations. Religionists may not be, as Jesus told the scribe, "far from the kingdom" (Mark 12:34). But probably the most large-scale and intensive explorations of the processes of temptation today are the work of psychotherapists.

There is another side to the secularization and specialization of our culture. If in many respects the secular specialist is closer to the kingdom than the religionists, this was true in the Judaism of Jesus' day. The churches shoot down ordered attention to temptation and emphasize sin and salvation. Their people focus on the righteousness of their particular memberships. They develop an inner circle that a person struggling with massive and significant temptation does not feel he or she can approach, much less be a part of. Instead, these persons go to self-help groups such as Adult Children of Alcoholics, Overeaters Anonymous, or other therapy programs for overstressed people. Or they seek help from psychiatrists, social workers, or psychologists. In the face of this dilemma, the American Association of Pastoral Counselors has become a vital force in translating faith-based understandings of human life from their psychological, sociological, and psychiatric terms. This task is important in order to give temptation-ridden and sin-laden people a place of safety where religious respectability is not a prerequisite for entry. These so-called secular settings become "cities of refuge" (see Num. 35:11–34). Even with the most open and compassionate church congregation, some problems are so complex they cannot be dealt with except in the highly antiseptic environments that professional therapists, including professional pastoral counselors, can provide.

A fourth and somewhat surprising purpose of this book came into focus after the first draft had been completed. In writing a second draft I began to realize that the biblical perspective of temptation is far more comprehensive than either personal piety or psychotherapeutic approaches to individual maturity can possibly encompass. This realization came while trying to grasp what temptation in the face of persecution was like for Christians of New Testament times and for persecuted and oppressed people today. Stories coming to light in South Africa, Eastern Europe, Central America, Afghanistan, and Russia describe Christian, Jewish, and Islamic persons suffering from repression and thus the temptation to renounce their faiths. In some countries psychotherapeutic diagnoses are used to "hospitalize" dissidents. The person who does not go along with the party line of the oppressors is considered to be mentally ill! Here the temptation is to avoid resistance "against the principalities, against the powers, against the world rulers of this present darkness, against the spiritual hosts of wickedness in the heavenly places" (Eph. 6:12). Any account of temptation that does justice to the biblical understanding must include this. Here, the psychological approach is less than adequate. We need to resort to life stories of people who have first-hand experience of this kind of temptation. This we will do in chapter 4.

1

Some Meanings of Temptation

One of my many promptings to write this book came in a letter from a person I do not know. She had just finished reading my book *Anxiety in Christian Experience,* published in 1955 and now out of print. She expressed appreciation for the book and said, "By the time I had completed the reading, the question came to mind if you had written a book on the nature of temptation in the Christian experience. . . . Now, after years of struggle with the idea and experience with the fact [of temptation], my hope is to find someone who also has worked through this dimension of spiritual reality as it relates to Christian experience and been able to verbalize it. Although a wealth of Scripture and experience come together in my reason that (for me) verify the imperative for the Christian to be cognizant in these matters, I have never been able to articulate them. If you have not written any such material, would you please wait before the Lord to see if He would have you do so?"

Oddly enough, I had been doing just that. Her letter seemed to be speaking not only the common experience of large numbers of people more inarticulate than she, it seemed to be a message from God to me as well. Thus, I feel the comradeship of the presence of God as, with fear and trembling, I explore the meanings of temptation. It is not a one-meaning reality.

The word temptation comes from the Latin *temptare* or *tentare,* which gives us the most commonly used meaning of temptation: "The action of being tempted, especially to evil; enticement, allurement, attraction." This kind of temptation is most vividly described by the author of the book of James (1:13–15):

Let no one say when he [or she] is tempted, "I am tempted by God"; for God cannot be tempted with evil and he himself tempts no one; but each person is tempted when he [or she] is lured and

enticed by his [or her] own desire. Then desire when it has conceived gives birth to sin; and sin when it is full-grown brings forth
death.

Temptation as Unlimited Desire

This text focuses attention first on temptation as springing
from our own desires. Notice that, although the book of James
in 2:19 refers to "demons [who] believe—and shudder," in the
passage in 1:13–15 no reference is made to the devil as the
source of temptation. Nor is God the one who tempts us. As
John H. Ropes, commenting on this passage, says (pp. 157–
158):

> It is highly significant that James' mind naturally turns for the true
> explanation of temptation not to the Jewish thought of Satan or of
> "the evil root," but to a psychological analysis. . . . The source of
> temptation is *desire,* and lies within, and not without, the man.

Consequently, we can assume a basic paradigm for understanding temptation: Self-deception is the parent evil of all
temptation.

Contemporary psychotherapists point to the universal human proneness to projection: that is, the process of throwing
upon others the impulses and thoughts that belong to oneself. A
person casts upon another intentions he or she considers undesirable, evil, and unworthy. As we will see in chapter 5, the
most vivid example of this temptation is found in the apostle
Paul's admonition in Galatians 6:1: "Brethren, if [someone] is
overtaken in any trespass, you who are spiritual should restore
him [or her] in a spirit of gentleness. Look to yourself, lest you
too be tempted." Self-examination precedes judgment of others and produces a spirit of gentleness.

Temptation begins within ourselves. It begins with the
desires of our own hearts. Modern psychotherapists would call
these desires "motives." Desires, or motives, generate in the
seedbed of our grand, unreal fantasies about ourselves. Three
such grandiose fantasies are most common: We fantasize that
we will not really die; we dream that there are no limits to what
is ours and what we can do; we imagine that we as individuals
and special-interest groups are the exception to all rules and
laws, even the law of gravity. Out of the deceptions of these
three fantasies, forbidden desires germinate, grow, and produce
bitter fruit all our lives.

Conventionally religious persons perceive desire to mean
sexual desire. Therefore the temptation of sex becomes, to

them, the sole meaning of temptation. However, sexual desire masks many other temptations, which beguile the mind more easily because of their mask of sexual desire. Sex can be a cover for the temptation to covet. Sex can be a means to gain power. Anger, unforgivingness, and sadism can mask themselves as sexual desire. The lust to win in a struggle of competition for prestige and status can use sexuality as a tool.

Biblical and psychological exploration blows the cover of sex. As Jeremiah says, "The heart is deceitful above all things." Yet he also says, "I the LORD search the mind and try the heart" (Jer. 17:9–10). Before we equate temptation with sexual desire, we must let God teach us what other desires are hiding beneath this cover. If, instead, we go ahead and equate temptation with sexual desire, we are, to use Isaiah's metaphor, on a bed "too short to stretch oneself on it, and the covering too narrow to wrap oneself in it" (Isa. 28:20). A much more adequate understanding of the luring and enticement of desire is necessary if we are to deal directly with our temptations, avoiding self-deception. The desire to be in God's place with no limits, to have all knowledge, and to be an exception to all other mortals, for example, rarely receives our attention. Pride separates us from the reality of our humanness, our ignorance, and our companionship in frailty with our fellow creatures.

Temptation as Excuse-making

A second kind of temptation is making excuses, and the excuse most often used to deceive ourselves about our temptations is to say bluntly, as James does, "I am tempted by God," instead of facing up to our own desires. When a severe stress or calamity comes upon us, we say God placed the trouble there. Most often it happened because such things happen to many people, and we are no exception to the laws of nature. Or we may be the makers of our own "bad luck." Let us say the bank forecloses on a mortgage on our house. With wisdom and foresight on our part this might not have happened.

Jesus spoke directly to the popular misconception of blaming God for temptation and catastrophic events. "There were those present at that very time who told him of the Galileans whose blood Pilate had mingled with their sacrifices. And he answered them, 'Do you think that these Galileans were worse sinners than all the other Galileans, because they suffered thus? I tell you, No; but unless you repent you will all likewise perish' " (Luke 13:1–3). To the pious Jew of Jesus' day, calamity was a result of God's punishment for sin. Galileans, to the Pharisees, were "generic sinners." "Can anything good come out of Nazareth?" Nathaniel asked about Jesus, a Galilean (John 1:46). Now these particular Galileans had been cut down by Pilate's soldiers while offering sacrifices. The Pharisees saw them as the worst sinners of all sinful Galilees. Not only did they blame God for the deaths, they made scapegoats of the Galileans. Thus they excused themselves from the rigorous self-examination of their own temptations, which had, as James puts it, become "full grown" and were about to bring forth their own death. He left them without an excuse.

Another excuse we use for covering over our temptations is to say that the Devil is responsible for them, not we ourselves. (One is faced here with the temptation to use one-verse interpretation and delete the teachings of the rest of the Old Testament concerning Satan as the tempter. To the contrary, this will be discussed at length in chapter 3.) The book of James does not mention Satan. Rather, James focuses on individual and community responsibility for human behavior: plans, desires, motives, impulses, and sins. In his view, we are not to put on some semblance of piety or cloak our temptations before the presence of almighty God, unto whom all hearts are opened and from whom no secrets are hid. We cannot add to God's knowledge of us by sharing with God our worst temptations. We have the choice between fellowship with God in our struggles with temptation and deceiving ourselves in lonely alienation from both God and our real selves. If we make the latter choice, a life of shame becomes the pattern of our lives. James insists that we ourselves take responsibility. We must not project the blame on either God or Satan.

This reference of mine to Satan is the first of many such references to come. The question always arises as to whether Satan is to be understood as a separate being or as a personification. Let me deal with this now. The Bible portrays Satan *both* as a being separate from human beings and as personified by human beings. The emphasis in this book is on the spiritual personifications of Satan. This is not to dodge the question of the separateness of the being of Satan. Rather, it is to deal with Satan existentially and not ontologically. In less technical language, my purpose is to deal with Satan at work in our own existence, not primarily as a being. Satan's being is counterfeit. Satan is not a being in the sense that God is a being. Satan's being is borrowed or stolen; it participates in unreality and deception.

As I have said, chapter 3 will deal with personifications of temptation. Suffice it to say here that Jesus named the devil as the parent of all deception. "When he lies, he speaks according to his own nature, for he is a liar and the father of lies" (John 8:44). James says that we are lured and enticed by our own desires. In *Paradise Lost* John Milton quotes the tempter in his plan to despoil God's creation, Adam and Eve (IV. 513–523):

> . . . All is not theirs, it seems:
> One fatal tree there stands, of knowledge called,
> Forbidden them to taste: Knowledge forbidden?
> Suspicious, reasonless. Why should their Lord
> Envy them that? Can it be sin to know,
> Can it be death? and do they only stand
> By ignorance, is that their happy state,
> The proof of their obedience and their faith? . . .
> Hence I will excite their minds
> With more desire to know.

Behind every desire there is a blind impulse that drives it. Milton insists that Satan is the deceiver who subtly turns the appropriate desire for knowledge into the greed-ridden desire for *all* knowledge. The paradox of responsibility says at one and the same time that Satan prompts temptation and we devise it ourselves. I prefer to follow James and say that we devise our own temptation. Satan is only our excuse. This made Eve and then Adam, as tradition has it, desire to be "equal with God." Prudential wisdom teaches us that "wisdom is the principal thing: therefore get wisdom: and with all thy getting get understanding" (Prov. 4:7, KJV). Understanding lets us know that we cannot get *all* knowledge. We are deceived into desiring all knowledge. Deception, both theologically and psychologically, particularly self-deception, is the parent evil.

Occasionally, in my care of profoundly psychotic persons, one of them will tell me, "I hear these voices that terrify me." I ask, "Are these voices the voice of one particular person?" They reply, "Yes. The devil tells me to kill myself." Such extreme commands also appear in other patients' reports. As their pastoral counselor, I respond with the question, "Do you know what Jesus said the devil is?" The answer is usually no. I respond, "Jesus said the devil is a liar. The truth is not in him. He is the father of lies." I encourage them to say this aloud when they hear voices. They tend to remember this godly admonition, use it, and be comforted as they do so. It is a workable admonition for all of us when we are tempted to blame our own desires on the devil.

Temptation as Spiritual Testing

A third kind of temptation is the testing of our faith in God, which happens in the common crises of human life and relationship. God created us in God's own image. In the process of our continuing creation, as we grow and mature as God created us to do, we are tested at many junctures of our pilgrimage. In this sense, God tests us, but not in the sense described by James and quoted at the start of this chapter, as we shall see later.

These temptations were focused on by the apostle Paul: "No temptation has overcome you that is not common to man. God is faithful, and he will not let you be tested beyond your strength, but with the temptation will provide the way of es- cape" (1 Cor. 10:13). The meaning of the Greek word used here for temptation, *peirasmos,* is rooted in the classical Greek words *peira,* a test or an attempt, and *peirazō,* to test or to tempt. These are the words from which we derive our words "experience" and "experiment."

Strange as it may seem, the testing concept of temptation is symbolized in the much-used idea of stress. Stress is a metaphor from the field of physics. How much weight in a building can a load-bearing pillar, beam, or set of bolts stand? The architect and the builder must know the answer to this question ahead of time. They must provide an ample margin of safety in the stress that the parts of the whole building can bear. God, the Architect of our being, also knows ahead of time how much we are able to bear.

Paul's message seems to be that it is God who has made us and not we ourselves. God is faithful to his creation. He will not allow or let or permit us to be tested beyond the strength he gives in his architectural design for us. He has already provided for us in creation and will continue to provide for us when we face temptation. He will provide a way of deliverance. God is faithful.

Does this mean God tests us? God created us in an order of creation in which the testing of our mettle as human beings is inevitable. Our creation thrusts us into a process in which we grow and mature. At each turning point in the pilgrimage of our maturity we can either regress, or fixate, or continue to grow. These turning points are times of testing of God's own design. In this sense God tests us. However, this is a very different form of testing from that referred to in James 1:12–15, as we have already seen.

The biblical story of the deliverance of the Hebrew people

from Egypt is a vivid example of God's intervention. They had been pushed to the limits of their resources by the Egyptians. Yet the real test of their character came in the wilderness travail, as they were born into and grew in their new sense of identity as the people of God under all sorts of trying circumstances. In giving the Ten Commandments, "Moses said to the people, 'Do not fear; for God has come to prove you, and that the fear of him may be before your eyes, that you may not sin' " (Ex. 20:20). The rigors of the wilderness, the crises of the course of their journey, were the proving ground of their identity as the people of God and of their character as participants in the unfolding story. Moses later instructs them to look back and "remember all the way which the LORD your God has led you these forty years in the wilderness, that he might humble you, testing you to know what was in your heart, whether you would keep his commandments, or not" (Deut. 8:2).

By analogy, let us say that all of us, as individuals and as communities of faith established in the name of God and our Lord Jesus Christ, live our lives as a pilgrimage. We may do so with clear commitments to covenants and promises we have made to God, ourselves, and others. Or we may refuse to form such covenants or make such promises. The crises of our personal and communal history become testing grounds for peeling off all deceptions, sifting out our real motives, and transforming our verbal commitments into the muscle and sinew of our very being and doing, rather than shrinking back in fear. This is the shaking of our foundations in which, as the book of Hebrews says, there is a "removal of what is shaken . . . in order that what cannot be shaken may remain" (Heb. 12:27).

Much pastoral counseling is crisis intervention. Crises are either developmental ones, such as marriage, the birth of a child, or retirement, or they are traumatic ones, such as the sudden death of a loved one, a divorce (either gradual or sudden), or an accident in which one or more persons are seriously injured. Each of these events can be of earthquake intensity in our world. Such order as we may have is thrown into chaos. Our presence of mind and our spiritual resources are placed under stress. Our capacity to stand steady, and not "cut and run" or resist, either literally or figuratively, is tested. We are being tempted as to whether we will face into the gathering storm or shrink back. As Hebrews says, "My righteous one shall live by faith, and if he shrinks back, my soul has no pleasure in him" (Heb. 10:38).

John Bunyan, in his book *Pilgrim's Progress,* told of Christian and Pliable setting out from the City of Destruction to the

Celestial City. They had not gone far before they stumbled and fell into the Slough of Despond. They were up to their necks in sludge. Pliable managed to get out first because he climbed out "the way that he already knew," which was on the side nearest the City of Destruction. He yielded to the temptation to shrink back. Christian, on the other hand, stayed in the mess until he could find the way out nearest the Celestial City. He moved by faith in the direction he had not yet gone but in which he had chosen to go.

Personality in individuals, families, and gathered communities either grows under the pressure of adversity or deteriorates. We must face adversity realistically, with faith. A courageous faith generates alternatives either for solution or for adaptation to the calamity. Without faith we shrink back in fear and chaos and begin generating excuses, blaming other people, bad luck, God, or the devil. The more the excuses proliferate, the more the person, family, or group becomes dysfunctional. In the language of Alcoholics Anonymous, our lives become unmanageable.

Which direction is taken in these testing crises is crucial. This is especially true when more than one person is involved, such as in a marriage. Concerted decision making is required. Self-absorption of married individuals and ever-present accusations of each other obscure all sense or vision of the direction the marriage is going. Such people are lost in the woods of their individual concerns. But the quintessence of temptation as testing is found in their decision making. They are faced with the choice of which path in the woods they will take. As Robert Frost says in "The Road Not Taken," "I took the one less traveled by, and that has made all the difference."

Temptation as the Anxiety of Low Aim

Much ethical disquietude manifests itself in a fourth temptation, anxious indecision, doing things against our better judgment—whether to take the *most* traveled road, take the easy way out, forfeit our high ideals for lower ones, and choose the immediate gratification of our desires rather than wait patiently for the longer-term satisfactions of life.

Martin Luther used a German term to name this kind of temptation: *Anfechtung.* Of this word, Roland Bainton said in *Here I Stand* (p. 42):

Before God the high and God the holy Luther was stupefied. For such an experience he had a word which has as much right to be carried over into English as *Blitzkrieg.* The word he used was

Anfechtung, for which there is no English equivalent. . . . It is all the doubt, turmoil, pang, tremor, panic, despair, desolation, and desperation which invade the spirit of man.

The meaning of *Anfechtung* is something of the story of Luther's life. *Anfechtung* involves the holy dread of being on our own before God, having our whole life in our hands and not knowing what to do with it. Yet we feel totally responsible to God to *decide* what to do with it. The issues are twofold: (1) Your faith in God—will you commit your life and destiny to God? (2) Your vocation—will you choose the high calling of God or will you pull away from faith in God and make a low-aim or very-low-aim choice? In this respect, C. W. Hovland ("*Anfechtung*," p. 46) quotes Luther: "I did not learn my theology all at once, but I had to search deeper for it where my temptations took me."

The tempting choice of a low-aim destiny or calling, if put into action, becomes sin in the biblical sense of missing the mark. The sense of despair arising from it is not a sense of guilt over specific acts committed. Rather, a sense of shame overwhelms us for not having become the person we could have been if we had aimed higher.

Temptation as Not Watching

A fifth form of temptation is not watching what we are doing or where we are going. This is rarely thought of as temptation, yet it is the cause of losing our clear sense of direction. By wandering, we fall into accidents, broken promises, quagmires of human relationships, and even life-threatening situations. As the process starts, the person is simply not watching; as it continues, the person is lulled into a false sense of security and a sleepy, dreamy lack of vigilance. Do not view this kind of temptation as a form of making excuses. It is not. Not watching is vastly different from those followers of Jesus who could not follow him because they had to bury their father or had just taken a wife. Not watching is more like being asleep when momentous decisions need to be made. In fact, Luke's account of the Transfiguration says, "Peter and those who were with him were heavy with sleep, and when they wakened they saw his glory and the two men [Moses and Elijah] who stood with him" (Luke 9:32). The apostle Paul associates it with death: "Awake, O sleeper, and arise from the dead, and Christ shall give you light" (Eph. 5:14). Excuse making is a conscious maneuver. Not watching is an unconscious "being out of it."

For example, few if any persons deliberately plan to become addicted to alcohol, drugs, destructive work habits, sexual liaisons with persons outside their marriage, gambling, or the misappropriation of money. The lost sheep has a history of wandering and not watching where it is going long before the Good Shepherd finds it. The person who most loudly protests his or her allegiance to Christ can just as easily be asleep at the wheel when the greatest danger of denying Christ is at hand.

Jesus went with his disciples to the garden of Gethsemane on the eve of his arrest. He asked them to wait while he went a little farther away from them to pray. He came back to them after agonizing in prayer. He found them asleep. He said to them, "Watch and pray that you may not enter into temptation; the spirit indeed is willing, but the flesh is weak" (Mark 14:38). Mark records that Jesus went to pray twice more. Each time, upon returning, he found the disciples asleep. They were neither praying nor watching for the danger threatening their teacher and themselves. The word translated as "watch" also means to be awake. Jesus' command is that we be alert, vigilant, and on guard.

The psychological skill implied here is the capacity to perceive real danger to ourselves or others. Another way of describing it is "the capacity of foresight." For many people, this capacity is either absent altogether or asleep at crucial times of danger. A good analogy is the capacity to feel real pain. In medical literature, fewer than one hundred patients have been recorded who do not have the capacity to feel pain. They are in constant danger from unfelt cuts, burns, and bruises. They do not feel hunger pains; there is no inner time clock to prompt these persons to eat. They lead lives of jeopardy, because pain, like temptation, is necessary to a normal existence. (See Oates and Oates, *People in Pain*.)

The normal function of pain is to awaken us, alert us, put us on guard against disease and injury. The normal psychological and spiritual function of the awareness of temptation is to put us on guard against the inherent dangers of sin.

Yet the nature of this kind of temptation is *not* to watch, *not* to test the spirit to see whether these things are of God or not, but to be naïve and gullible about what kinds of danger lurk in the smooth sales talk of our marketing world. Jesus called us to "be wise as serpents and innocent as doves" (Matt. 10:16). We are too soon old and too late smart, as the Pennsylvania Dutch say. We are conned and taken in too easily by today's peddlers of pious but ethically empty religion. Our pain sensors, our capacity for watching our step, are too frequently not alert to seductive salesmen selling religious paint jobs. They permit Satan permanent residence in their silk-suited bodies.

In heeding Jesus' admonition to watch and pray lest we enter into temptation, we are not without companionship. Paul tells us that "the peace of God, which is beyond our utmost understanding, will keep guard over your hearts and your thoughts, in Christ Jesus" (Phil. 4:7, NEB). This presence of the peace of God both chastened and challenged the apostle Peter when he denied knowing Christ. Jesus told him he would be sifted by Satan; he also reassured and commissioned him. "Simon, Simon, behold, Satan demanded to have you, that he might sift you like wheat, but I have prayed for you that your faith may not fail; and when you have turned again, strengthen your brethren" (Luke 22:31–32). And events happened in that order. Peter's motives were sifted. He yielded to temptation when he was not watching or feared he was being watched by the persecutors. He "turned again," when he saw the risen Christ, and strengthened the other disciples.

This chapter has discussed five forms of temptation: the living enticement of our own undisciplined desires, the wide array of excuses we generate to justify our behavior, the spiritual testings that are common to all of us, the temptation of low aim in settling for less than our better judgment suggests for our life, and the selective inattention of not watching where we are going and what we are doing. In varying contexts, these meanings will reappear in the succeeding chapters.

2

The Most Subtle Temptation

Subtlety—that is, deceit, cunning, or treachery—character-izes the least conscious of our temptations. These temptations are like the nose on one's face. People who know us may say, "That is as plain as the nose on your face." But however plain our noses may be to them, we cannot see them very well. We can look in a mirror, but, as the book of James says, when we go away, we "at once" forget what we are like (James 1:24). Hence we can deceive ourselves. When we are flattered or ma-ligned, when we take too seriously the praise or criticism of others, we can be subtly deceived by others as well.

Many Christians loudly protested the release of a movie enti-tled *The Last Temptation of Christ.* This temptation, according to the movie, appears to Jesus in a dream in which he is mak-ing love to Mary Magdalene and hoping to have children. His waking temptation is to set up an earthly kingdom and be a political power in his own right. The irony of both the moviemakers and the Christian protesters is that they focus not on the last temptation of Jesus but probably the first one, along with the temptation to turn stones into bread when he had fasted for forty days. This was the temptation of the greed for power suffered by him who "in every respect has been tempted as we are, yet without sin" (Heb. 4:15).

Greed to take God's place, then, is the most subtle of all temptations, the one of which we are least aware. Because of this unawareness, this is the most intense and persistent of un-disciplined desires. Here is an illustration.

As the chaplain at a large mental hospital, I was preparing for evening vespers one Sunday afternoon when a knock came at the door. It was a woman about forty-five years of age. She introduced herself. "I am your God. I have come to tell you what to say to the people of God." I invited her to have a seat and said in response, "You are indeed made in the image of

God, as I am also. But you are not God and neither am I. We are only messengers of God. What is your message from God?"

This person has always impressed me because, though she was deceiving herself, she was more honest with me than many so-called "normal" people about this subtlest of temptations—to take God's place, to have all power, to delude ourselves into thinking we are omnipotent. We are tempted as Jesus was: "And the devil took him up, and showed him all the kingdoms of the world in a moment of time, and said to him, 'To you I will give all this authority and their glory; for it has been delivered to me, and I will give it to whom I will. If you, then, will worship me, it shall all be yours'" (Luke 4:5–7). Jesus, in his hunger and exhaustion from forty days in the wilderness, resisted the temptation in behalf of the worship of the God of truth rather than the worship of the father of lies. The driving desire behind this temptation is the desire for power and personal, ecclesiastical, or national glory.

At risk in this source of temptation is a person's, church's, or nation's relationship to God. Milton states it well in describing Satan, the rebellious angel who, seeking a corporate takeover in heaven, was cast into hell, a territory prepared for him (*Paradise Lost* I. 261–263):

> Here we may reign secure, and in my choice
> To reign is worth ambition though in hell:
> Better to reign in hell, than serve in heaven.

Milton based his long poem in part on Revelation 12:9, which recounts the war in heaven in which "the great dragon was thrown down, that ancient serpent, who is called the Devil and Satan . . . he was thrown down to the earth, and his angels were thrown down with him." The major difference between the Bible and Milton at this point is that the Bible portrays Satan as being let loose on earth. Milton says he was cast into hell, which was designed especially for him. This is an aside, however, from the central issue of the war in heaven, on which both agree, the struggle for ultimate power and authority that Satan and his followers waged against God. For them the temptation to defeat and vanquish God is not subtle. Satan's subtlety only appears later in the garden of Eden. The tools of open warfare were laid aside, it seems, and deception, cleverness, and cunning were used instead. Revelation describes Satan as "the deceiver of the whole world" (12:9).

Much later than Milton, Friedrich Nietzsche (1844–1900), the German formulator of the superman philosophy, describes the limitlessness of the desire for power even more vividly as people's ambition to annihilate—yes, to kill—God. Then they could become God! In his book *Joyful Wisdom* (p.168), he describes this desire: "God is dead! God remains dead! We have killed him! How shall we console ourselves, the most murderous of murderers? . . . Shall we not ourselves have to become gods, merely to seem worthy of it?"

Nietzsche lays bare the desire to be God. This was the desire with which Eve and then Adam were tempted. They should not eat of the tree, God told them, lest they die. "But the serpent said to the woman, 'You will not die. For God knows that when you eat of it your eyes will be opened, and you will be like God, knowing good and evil' " (Gen. 3:4–5). John Calvin, in his commentary on Genesis (pp. 150–151), says Satan "censures God as being moved by jealousy, and as having given the command concerning the trees, for the purpose of keeping man in an inferior rank. . . . I have no doubt that Satan promises them *divinity*." Yet the desire for all knowledge was there before Satan, and the feeling of inferior rank to God and between each other preceded the temptation. Especially, Milton says, was this true in Eve's mind before she shared the fruit with Adam. He imagines her inner reflections (*Paradise Lost* IX. 816–826):

> . . . But to Adam in what sort
> Shall I appear? Shall I to him make known
> As yet my change, and give him to partake
> Full happiness with me, or rather not,
> But keep the odds of knowledge in my power
> Without Copartner? so to add what wants
> In Female sex, the more to draw his Love,
> And render me more equal, and perhaps,
> A thing not undesirable, sometime
> Superior: for, inferior, who is free?

"Keeping the odds of knowledge in my power without Copartner"—that is Eve's most subtle temptation. Only *she* would be a goddess. She did not, however, yield to the temptation. She resolved: "Adam shall share with me in bliss or woe: So dear I love him, that with him all deaths I could endure, without him live no life" (*Paradise Lost* IX. 830–834). To be tempted is not to sin; yielding is sin. As Martin Luther says in *The Large Catechism* (p. 78), "To feel temptation, therefore, is a quite different thing from consenting and yielding to it. We must all feel it, though not all to the same degree; some have more frequent and severe temptation than others."

Our present crisis as individuals, churches, and nations is a *knowledge* revolution. This is an information era. Knowledge is power, influence, and money. The subtle temptation is: "Master all the information of Wall Street [the CIA, MI5, the KGB] and you shall be as God. God will be irrelevant; you will have all power." The subtle illusion that we can conquer, replace, or even slay God is a deceptive source of our temptations. This illusion infiltrates personal decision making, family relationships, bureaucratic decision making, national policy-making, and international intrigue. Eve's struggle with the allure of knowledge is a struggle common to us all.

These interacting forces within a Christian community present both pastors and lay persons with the subtle temptation to lord it over one another. The Bible easily becomes the center of power struggles as to whose interpretation will prevail. The seminaries and the publishing houses become objects of criticism by pastors of churches and lay persons. Such controversies easily become theater-of-the-absurd expressions of the self-elevation of leaders who do what they do and feel that they do God a service. Rarely do deacons hear a confession that someone "knows in part and prophesies in part" (see 1 Cor. 13:9, KJV).

The test of character—in other words, the temptation—of highly educated teachers of the Bible, those called to make this a lifelong profession, is how to maintain integrity in the face of attacks by pastors and lay persons who assail their fidelity to the Bible, their right to be employed by the denomination, and even their sincerity as Christians.

In order to keep our head in such conflicts, we must be committed to being edifying spirits: that is, to build up persons in the community of faith rather than pull them down, tear them apart, and eliminate them. Just as a clock that won't run is right twice a day, all people, no matter how "wrong, wrong, wrong" they may be, are right some of the time. The laconic wisdom of the Orient speaks volumes: "The gift of my enemy to me is that portion of the truth he has which I do not have." We can learn something from that person if we are committed to building up, not tearing down. To do this we must be open to discovering when others are right.

The major need in the face of the temptations we encounter in the middle of major social conflicts of any kind is an antidote to the temptation. The antidote is to have a clear personal identity that is nurtured by an even clearer sense of mission. Our mission demands that both our goals in the ministry of teaching and counseling and the means for achieving those goals shall convey clearly the mind "which is yours in Christ Jesus" (Phil. 2:5). No other option is workable. To search for his appearance and presence in all relationships demands that we not indulge our need to play God in other people's lives. This does not remove temptation. To the contrary, this devotion both defines and accentuates the intensity of temptation. As Martin Luther says, in commenting on Psalm 127 (p. 269), "the desire and the presumption to be like unto God, which is in us and begun in Paradise, cannot be shaken off, no, not in the saints or the children of God."

However, a firm and clear sense of mission does loosen the grip of this desire and transform it into service to those who are hungry, thirsty, strangers, naked, sick, or in prison. We are enabled, as Proverbs 4:23–27 suggests:

> Keep your heart with all vigilance;
>   for from it flow the springs of life.
> Put away from you crooked speech,
>   and put devious talk far from you.
> Let your eyes look directly forward,
>   and your gaze be straight before you.
> Take heed to the path of your feet,
>   then all your ways will be sure.
> Do not swerve to the right or to the left;
>   turn your foot away from evil.

The indwelling mind of Christ transforms the lust for power into a love to serve rather than rule. His mind changes the grandiose rejection of our human limitations into a joyful human acceptance of these boundaries. This puts us in fellowship rather than in competition with our fellow human beings. It humbles arrogant know-nothings and know-it-alls of whatever creed, color, or sex. Such a person sincerely and persistently seeks the knowledge of God in the face of Jesus Christ, wherever manifestations of that knowledge may be found.

The Subtle Temptation of "Being Helpful"

A psychotherapeutic adage says, "Run like mad when tempted to help!" A psychiatrist in Boston once told a group of us, "If you feel like you have to help someone, stop first and reexamine your compulsion to help until you no longer are driven to do so. Then you are ready to combine wisdom with your help." These two statements imply that certain kinds of "help" are subtle violations of the personhood of the people to whom help is extended. In terms of Christian moral theology, we would say that such helpfulness *sins* against the persons being helped. Before the impulse can be a temptation, sin must be a potential action, however subtle and deceptive it may appear.

The need to help, then, is not a pure unadulterated need to serve others. It is the crude ore (or oil) that needs refining through soul-searching and spiritual discipline. It is generously contaminated with the fantasy of our all-powerfulness, the desire to control even the smallest details of other people's lives, the desire to take God's place in other people's lives. In the final analysis, the people we are trying to help become a means to our self-gratification instead of persons in their own right under God. We foster the dependency of the willing ones and declare as hopeless those who resist. Resistance, contrary to much psychological moralization, is not always bad. It may be a cry for freedom from us, the "helper."

One biblical personality who struggled with this temptation to play God in the lives of his family was Joseph, son of Jacob, as recorded in Genesis 37 and 39–50. At the age of seventeen, Joseph was the best beloved son of Jacob. He was preferred even more than his brothers by his father because "he was the son of his old age." This amounted to rejection of the other sons. They hated Joseph "and could not speak peaceably to him" (Gen. 37:3–4).

As if this were not enough, Joseph added fuel to the fire of their hatred by telling them of at least two dreams he had. In the first they were binding sheaves of grain in the field and all his brothers' sheaves bowed down to his sheaf. In the second dream, the sun, the moon, and eleven stars bowed down to him. In this dream, he went further; he told his father and his brothers. Jacob rebuked him, saying, "What is this dream that you have dreamed? Shall I and your mother and your brothers indeed come to bow ourselves to the ground before you?" (Gen. 37:10). This scene closes with the statement: "And his brothers were jealous of him, but his father kept the saying in mind" (Gen. 37:11).

The brothers plotted to kill him, but first they stripped him and threw him into a deep pit to die of starvation and exposure to the elements. Then they relented and sold him to a caravan of Ishmaelites on their way to Egypt. This scene ends with his brothers telling Jacob that Joseph had been torn to pieces by a wild beast. Jacob wept and mourned his son.

The next several scenes describe Joseph's gradual ascent to power in the Egyptian pharaoh's court, helped by his ability to interpret dreams. After earlier experiences in the pit, in slavery, and in prison, he never told anyone else his dreams: that is, if he had any dreams he could remember. Rather, he said to

those who needed interpretations of their dreams, "Do not interpretations belong to God? Tell them to me, I pray you"
(Gen. 40:8). He has not yet made a clear distinction between
himself and God. That will require more time and suffering on
Joseph's part.

His capacity as an interpreter of dreams brought him finally
to Pharaoh, who had a dream through which Joseph predicted
famine in the land. Joseph became Pharaoh's preferred adviser
and his minister of agriculture through seven years of plenty
and seven years of famine. Enter the coalition of power with
the pharaoh!

The focal scenes of this story tell of Joseph's brothers coming
to Egypt to ask for famine relief. They did not recognize him at
first. Joseph used his power to make them fear for their lives.
He put them all in prison, except one, on the condition that the
one would go home and bring back the youngest brother, Benjamin. He jailed them on suspicion of being spies. Then he let
all but one go back to their father. At least they too now knew
what prison was like. Now, could they remember having put
him in a pit? How sweet revenge can be at first! But revenge is a
kind of wild justice that operates outside reason and law. Joseph's manipulations, however, continued to exact this wild
justice of his brothers. He hid his own silver goblet in Benjamin's sack. Then, when the brothers had not gone very far on
their journey home, he sent his servants to recapture them.
They were brought back for him to accuse them of having stolen the goblet. He threatened the life of the one in whose sack it
was found. It was found in Benjamin's sack. What a cruel ma-
nipulation to demonstrate Joseph's power! The trick completed, Joseph permitted them to go on their way.

This took them a good while because Jacob, or Israel, was
loath to let them have Benjamin. Finally he permitted them to
return with Benjamin along with a load of gifts to placate "the
man," Joseph. When they arrived in Egypt and in Joseph's
presence again, Judah, fearing that Benjamin would be held
hostage, made an intercessory plea, asking that if his brother
Benjamin was to be held hostage, that he himself be held in
Benjamin's stead: "For how can I go back to my father if the
lad is not with me? I fear to see the evil that would come upon
my father" (Gen. 44:34). In *Genesis 37–50,* Claus Westermann
says of this remarkable event (pp. 137–138):

> Here . . . the Bible speaks for the first time of vicarious suffering.
> . . . God has discovered the brothers' guilt; hence, one of them
> offers himself as a slave in a foreign land in place of the youngest.
> . . . There is a path that leads from the Joseph story right up to the

threshold of the community; the healing of a breach is possible only when there is one who is ready to take the suffering upon oneself.

What an impact Judah's offer had upon Joseph! He forsook his manipulative game of revenge, broke into tears, and said, "I am Joseph: is my father still alive?" (Gen. 45:3). He no longer had them bow down to him, although his dream when he was seventeen actually had come true; he had the power of life and death over them. It tempted and tested him for a while. He tempted and tested them for a while. It seems, however, the sacrificial example of his brother, Judah, who had interceded with the brothers at the pit not to kill him but to sell him into slavery, had transformed his need for revenge into compassion for fellowship with his brothers.

Joseph's long-held-back tears, though, seem to have washed out this desire to play God in their lives. Instead he takes the identity of the brother and servant of his brothers. He attributes the whole history of their dealings with one another to the farseeing providence of God: "I am your brother, Joseph, whom you sold into Egypt. And now do not be distressed, or angry with yourselves, because you sold me here; for God sent me before you to preserve life" (Gen. 45:4–5). Later, after the death of his father, he is tempted again. His brothers "came and fell down before him, and said, 'Behold, we are your servants.'" Then Joseph puts his temptation—no longer subtle—into words: "Fear not, for am I in the place of God?" (Gen. 50:18–19).

His omnipotent feelings and need for vengeance have been laid aside. He gives God homage as the all-wise, all-powerful Providence. He has become not God but the servant of his brothers and an instrument of God's grace.

However, the irony of Joseph's helpfulness to his family shows up in Exodus 1:8–14. His "help" was still contingent upon the Egyptian pharaoh's power. When that pharaoh was gone and another arose "who did not know Joseph," he enslaved the Hebrews and "set taskmasters over them to afflict them with heavy burdens" (Ex. 1:8, 11).

The Tyranny of Family Secrets

The intriguing family history of Joseph, his brothers, and their father illustrates vividly the deception and tragedy that take place when secrets rule the life of the family. That was true in Joseph's family. It is true in families today. If the secret involves matters of life and death, as in the case of Joseph's brothers showing Joseph's bloodstained coat to their father and letting him conclude that a wild beast has devoured his son, then yielding to the temptation of deception will be a lifelong burden to carry. A contemporary example of this is the way some adoptive parents keep the fact of the adoption a secret from the adopted child. The issue of family secrets exemplifies our proneness to the most subtle temptation of putting oneself in God's place in the lives of others.

Family therapists today take seriously the presence of family secrets as tyranny of one or more family members over the rest of the family. As Edwin Friedman says in *Generation to Generation* (pp. 52–53), "The communication system of many families is riddled with secrets." He says that secrets divide a family, create estrangements and false liaisons in a family, distort family members' perceptions of one another, and make any problems the family has to face all the more difficult. The chronic anxiety that secrets generate kills the integrity of the whole family system.

Major crises, such as famine in the case of Joseph's family, tend to expose previously kept secrets. Secrets are kept alive by cunning, deception, and the grandiosity of one or more family members yielding to the subtlest of temptations to exercise total control over the rest of the family. They initiate a family game that is kept alive by deception.

Life's crises have a way of calling off the game in agonizing moments of truth. The subtly concealed God complex of the most powerful member of the family, the holder of the secret, as in the case of Joseph, is challenged. Joseph had all the secrets in his hands. When the whole family came to crisis at his father's death, he said, "Fear not, for am I in the place of God? As for you, you meant evil against me; but God meant it for good, to bring it about that many people should be kept alive, as they are today. So do not fear; I will provide for you and your little ones" (Gen. 50:19–21). The anxiety evaporated when the power of the secret was relinquished in the period of grief after their father's death.

The members of dysfunctional families today carry secrets from each other. Addictions such as alcoholism, drug abuse, and credit-card mismanagement are often hidden in a conspiracy of silence and secrecy to protect the rest of the family from embarrassment. Extramarital affairs thrive on secrecy. One parent may conspire for a daughter to have an abortion and keep the secret from the rest of the family.

Probably the most common family secret is incest. The parent who sexually abuses another member of the family usually swears that person to secrecy, often with severe threats if the person should break silence. Sometimes the threat is more subtle and controlling, as James Leehan says in *Pastoral Care for Survivors of Family Abuse* (p. 28):

> Often the trusted authority figure does not force the child into sexual activity. He cajoles, tricks, or kindly manipulates the child into a sexual relationship. . . . It is "what you do to be nice to your uncle."
>
> But another message is added soon after the act is performed. "This is something just between us. This is not something we want to tell anyone else. It is our little secret."

The clutch of dire circumstance has a way of squeezing the family secret out of its hiding place. Life challenges the omnipotence of the holders of the secret. Truth has a way of making itself known in spite of our illusions of all-powerfulness. As Jesus said, "For nothing is hid that shall not . . . be known and come to light" (Luke 8:17).

The creative alternative to the deception of family secrets is that the family include in their covenant of love the commitment to face together whatever has to be faced. This rules out the tyranny of one member over the whole family system. It challenges the temptation of any one member of the family to manipulate and control the rest for his or her own purposes.

Narcissism and the Subtlest Temptation

The core psychological component of the subtlest temptation—the temptation to play, replace, or do away with God—is narcissism. The narcissistic person has an exaggerated sense of self-importance and is preoccupied with fantasies of unlimited success, power, and brilliance. A sense of entitlement pervades the narcissist's dealings with other people. The amount of self-deception involved in this is difficult to overestimate. We are not talking here about the benign narcissism of infants and children. We are talking about chronic adult narcissism, a person who lives with an inflated self-admiration, an absence of empathy for others, an arrogant unflappableness, and a pervasive sense of being entitled to do whatever he or she wishes. The person is devoid of real gratitude because anything anyone does for him or her is considered to be well deserved and only what the person was owed anyway.

The glory of humankind is that we are made in the image of God. As Paul Tillich says in *Systematic Theology* (II, pp. 50–

51), this "structured centeredness" gives us our "greatness, dignity, and being." "But this perfection is, at the same time, man's temptation. Man is tempted to make himself existentially the center of himself and his world." This is hubris, or self-elevation. "It is distinctly expressed in the serpent's promise to Eve that eating from the tree of knowledge will make man equal with God. . . . *Hubris* is the self-elevation of man into the sphere of the divine."

Blatant examples of self-elevation are evident in such historical figures as Hitler, Nero, Caligula, and others like them who have unleashed their terror on the earth. These are deranged examples of narcissism, as in the case of Jim Jones, who elevated himself to the position of pronouncing a death sentence for the more than nine hundred followers who obeyed his command in Guyana to take cyanide-laced Kool-Aid and die. These are not subtle; they are notorious and flagrant sinners above all others who make the rest of us feel pious in contrast.

However, the subtle deceptiveness of the temptation of narcissism in political and church leaders who sell wholesale their self-elevation to power often goes undetected by them and their devoted dependents. "Suffering servant" martyrs who "only want to be helpful" but who reduce a family member to abject dependence may not only go unnoticed in their self-elevation but may actually applaud themselves and be praised by those who know the story. The self-elevating uses of conventional "righteousness" stagger the imagination. Writing in the face of the subtlest temptation of hubris, one turns abruptly to Paul's admonition: "Examine yourselves, to see whether you are holding to your faith. Test yourselves. Do you not realize that Jesus Christ is in you?—unless indeed you fail to meet the test!" (2 Cor. 13:5).

The test is our need and temptation to dominate others. How much do we need to be in total control of those around us? How ready are we to arrive at an act of surrender in which we admit our helplessness? With what kind of abandon can we rely upon God at work in the circumstances of life to activate the responsible freedom of those we are determined to control, manipulate, and render weak and ineffectual? This calls not for rage toward the "helpee." It requires, instead, empathy for the way one's controlling behavior weakens and takes strength away from the other person. When we admit our helplessness, we begin to invest confidence and self-esteem in others.

This act of surrender can be seen as a moment or series of moments when persons inflated by illusions of total control, defiance, and grandiosity actually cease to function effectively.

If and when that happens, the narcissist is opened up to reality. He or she can listen and learn without conflict, arrogance, and fighting back. He or she gains a sense of relatedness to other people. Both "helper" and "helpee" can admit in the depths of their being the limitations, helplessness, and weakness of their humanity. They are now in a state of confession; ceasing to fight life, they accept life. They are ready for the guidance of the wisdom of God and the power of the presence of God; they no longer need to play, replace, or destroy God. The surges of unconscious desire to be God give way to a peaceful serenity that glorifies God and enjoys God's presence daily.

Even more completely human than this act of surrender is the acceptance of the limitations of what we can do. Whether we are the "know-it-all" or the "know-nothing" preacher, a Joseph or a Josephine, someone who dreams of others bowing down to him or her or a family member who decides to be the ultimate rescuer, we find it a severe task to admit our finiteness, our limitations, and our helplessness.

When we reach the end of the tether of our built-in limitations, we are indeed, as Tennyson said, like infants "crying in the night . . . and with no language but a cry." Yet the God we know in Jesus Christ became such an infant, who lived and labored under the same finite limits we do, grew, and was crucified, buried, and raised again. He sent the Holy Spirit, who makes intercession for us in struggles of our spirits that are too deep for words.

3

Personifications
of Temptation

Temptation to do wrong or to fantasize persistently about doing wrong does not occur in a vacuum. Temptation happens within and between persons. Evil personifies itself, and temptation comes to us either in mental images or in the actual presence of persons. This sounds quite abstract until we mention the personage known as the tempter (Matt. 4:3; 1 Thess. 3:5) or Satan, the devil, the dragon, or the ancient serpent (Rev. 2:9–10; 12:9, 12–17; 20:2). Then suddenly the personification of temptation becomes concrete.

The paradigm of meanings of temptation that applies most specifically to the personification of evil is the temptation to make excuses. When we think of Satan, the most obvious temptation is to blame Satan for our inner struggle against evil. Satan becomes our excuse for everything. Excuse making is the stock-in-trade of the personifications of evil.

This, however, raises a question that was dealt with in chapter 1, at the outset of this discussion: Is Satan as a personification not a being "in himself," or are evil persons incarnations of Satan? This has been briefly considered by saying that in scripture Satan is a character depicted both as an agent and as an adversary of God. Jesus encountered Satan as an independent spirit and as an incarnation within persons. Furthermore, we experience evil both as self-generated distorted desires and as being acted upon by the tempter. Often these work together.

However, remember that the "being" of Satan is a counterfeit of reality, copied, borrowed, or stolen from God's being. None of these are with God's permission. Satan's being is the quintessence of unreality.

Let us dare to think, then, that the tempter, Satan, the devil as depicted in the scripture is a counterfeiter of the Lord God's manner of revealing himself to us: Satan *incarnates* himself in the form of persons. However, he does so in his own particular way. Jesus "did not count equality with God a thing to be grasped" (Phil. 2:6). Satan is not interested in equality with God but in replacing God to become "the god of this world" (2 Cor. 4:4). Jesus "emptied himself, taking the form of a servant, being born in the likeness" of persons (Phil. 2:7). Satan inflates himself and, in the likeness of a person, enchants us with power, people, substances, and fantasies. Jesus "humbled himself and became obedient unto death, even death on a cross" (Phil. 2:8). Satan incarnates himself in human beings, so we become arrogant and self-elevated. We assume we are immortal, exempt from death. We set up kingdoms that are to last for "a thousand years" (2 Peter 3:8). What a chasm of difference, even as the personification of temptation to evil works on the same principle of incarnation and personification that God's revelation of himself in Jesus Christ does.

As Shakespeare so aptly describes men—and women—in *Measure for Measure* (II.2.117–122):

> . . . but man, proud man,
> Drest in a little brief authority,
> Most ignorant of what he's most assur'd,
> His glassy essence, like an angry ape,
> Plays such fantastic tricks before high heaven
> As make the angels weep; who, with our spleens,
> Would all themselves laugh mortal.

Seen from a psychological point of view, this corresponds to the difference between what Gordon Allport calls "egoistic" interests and "altruistic" interests. Altruism comes about by a "genuine transmutation of interests"; it is not "simply a varnish laid over personality" (*Personality,* p. 169). Or, if we speak in terms of the personality disorders we carry in our being, the psychiatric descriptions are filled with ethical implications and assumptions. For example, note the differences between the narcissist, devoid of empathy, and the noncompulsive person, who is wholeheartedly committed as an accurately empathic and wisely caring person in relation to other people. These are results of character choices made in late adolescence and early adulthood. As Scott Peck says in *People of the Lie* (p. 77), "The essential psychological problem of human evil, I believe, is a particular variety of human evil."

Temptation is the testing ground for these claims of God and Satan. Temptation is the battleground of character as we exercise our freedom to choose whom we will serve. Both God and Satan stand at the door and knock. We hear both voices and decide which we will let enter and be incarnated in our being.

This personification of temptation is dramatized in many instances in the biblical story.

The Serpent

Nowhere in the Genesis 3 account of the temptation and fall of Adam and Eve do the words tempter, Satan, or the devil appear. Only the serpent, "more subtle than any other wild creature that the LORD God had made" (v. 1), is mentioned as the agent of temptation. Christian tradition gets the description of Satan as personified or incarnated in the serpent from Revelation 20:2, which speaks of "that ancient serpent, who is the Devil and Satan." However, the original account in Genesis does not make this distinction. There the tempter is the serpent only.

Genesis 3 describes the serpent as most subtle. It also notes that the serpent was one of God's creatures, a part of the creation God found to be good. In fact, in the succeeding accounts of scripture (Num. 21:6–9), the serpent was an agent of both death and healing. The fiery serpents first bit the people and caused them to die. Then God ordered Moses to make a fiery serpent out of bronze and set it upon a pole. Then if a person bitten by a serpent looked at the bronze serpent, he or she would live. The lifting up of Jesus on the cross is likened, in John 3:14, to the lifting up of the serpent by Moses in the wilderness. The healing dimension of the symbol of the serpent is made irrelevant by Christ's death on the cross.

In Greek mythology, the serpent also appears as an agent of healing. Asclepius, or Aesculapius in Latin, was a son of Apollo. He learned medicine from a centaur and became so skilled in healing that he could revive the dead, whereupon Zeus killed him. Apollo then persuaded Zeus to make his son the god of medicine. The Greeks built temples for the worship of Asclepius, and physicians treated people in these temples. They identified themselves by carrying a staff with two entwined snakes. That serpentine symbol still lives today in the caduceus insignia of the medical profession.

Returning to the biblical account of the serpent, in 2 Kings 18:4 we are told that Hezekiah in his reforms "broke in pieces the bronze serpent that Moses had made."

In the biblical story, also, the serpent is commended by Jesus in Matthew 10:16 when he advises his disciples to "be wise as serpents and innocent as doves" because he was sending them out as sheep among wolves. The serpent is also a test of faith in the "addition" to Mark's Gospel of Mark 16:9–20. The Great Commission here is accompanied by a promise and a prediction in which Jesus is reported as saying, "They will pick up serpents, and if they drink any deadly thing, it will not hurt them" (v. 18). There is no reference here to Satan as being incarnate in the serpent.

Not so John Milton. He took the personification of the Devil and Satan in the serpent at face value and described vividly in poetic rhythms how this incarnation took place. In *Paradise Lost* (IX.161–169) he depicts the Devil as facing the necessity of incarnating himself into the being of the serpent:

> . . . [I] glide obscure, and pry
> In every bush and brake, where hap may find
> The serpent sleeping, in whose mazy folds
> To hide me and the dark intent I bring.
> O foul descent! that I, who erst contended
> With gods to sit the highest, am now constrained
> Into a beast, and mixed with bestial slime,
> This essence to incarnate and imbrute,
> That to the height of deity aspired!
> But what will not ambition and revenge
> Descend to?

Satan, Job's Tempter and Tester

The first assembly in heaven of God and the sons of God (who apparently made up a celestial court around the Lord) either had a visitor in Satan or possibly an irregular attendant at the council. In this instance, there was no incarnation of Satan in another form. However, in *The Book of Job* (p. 89), Norman C. Habel questions the use of "the Satan" in this passage. He says that *haśśāṭān*

> is not the personal name Satan but a role specification meaning "the accuser/adversary/doubter." . . . The verbal root *śṭn* does not refer to an action which is necessarily evil but to the behavior of one who opposes or challenges another party. . . . In the court context of Zech. 3:1–2 the Satan seems to hold the office of a prosecutor intent on establishing justice.

Contextually, then, we may see Satan here as a prosecuting attorney. However, evil design seems to be absent. In Job, Satan seems to work as God's legal representative, if only momentarily. It is conventional wisdom to assume that all biblical references depict Satan as evil. But close study does not bear this out.

However, Job is turned over to Satan by God to be tested.

The meaning of temptation as a testing of Job's moral and spiritual fiber is definitely present. It is almost as if Satan is an investigative lawyer who sets up his own sting operation to test Job's integrity. In this sense, the testing is a covert operation and Satan has the approval of the Chief Executive Officer. If this hypothesis is right, we can assume that here is a variation of the incarnation theme. Then Satan goes under cover.

After Job 2:7–8, Satan does not appear in this book except incarnate in the actions of Job's wife and those of his friends, Eliphaz the Temanite, Bildad the Shuhite, and Zophar the Naamathite. They certainly embody the testing inquisition and disputation with Job, but it is a stretch of the imagination to consider Job's wife and his three friends as incarnations of Satan. However, the mystery still remains as to why he disappears from the drama of Job's testing.

Satan in Jesus' Experience

Satan appears in a double perspective in the experience of Jesus. He is both a separate spirit or presence and is incarnated in people. The Matthew and Luke accounts of the temptations of Jesus in the wilderness depict the Holy Spirit leading him into the wilderness "to be tempted by the devil" (Matt. 4:1). The core temptation seems to be the one in which "the devil took him to a very high mountain, and showed him all the kingdoms of the world and the glory of them" that Jesus could have if he would fall down in worship. Here Jesus addresses him as Satan: "Begone, Satan! for it is written, 'you shall worship the Lord your God and him only shall you serve' " (Matt. 4:8–10).

Here was a test as to who God is and whether or not Satan could enter into Jesus and take over his life by offering him all the power and glory on earth. Jesus would have counterfeit power. He was choosing whether or not he wanted to be a pawn because he himself would be under the rule of Satan and serve as a proxy for the god of this world. The dramatic difference here is that Jesus did not offer Satan a dwelling place. He forced him to stand outside as the evil spirit he is.

However, the devil did not just vanish from existence; he "departed from him until an opportune time" (Luke 4:13). At least one of those opportune times was when Jesus and his disciples were at Caesarea Philippi. Satan, Jesus recognized, had incarnated himself in Simon Peter, who sought to dissuade Jesus from the path to the crucifixion. "But he turned and said to Peter, 'Get behind me, Satan! You are a hindrance to me; for you are not on the side of God, but of men' " (Matt. 16:23). Later, just before the crucifixion, Jesus said to Peter, "Simon, Simon, behold, Satan demanded to have you, that he might sift you like wheat, but I have prayed for you that your faith may not fail; and when you have turned again, strengthen your brethren" (Luke 22:31–32).

The success of Satan in embodying himself in one of the disciples, Peter, was thus frustrated by the prayers of Jesus. Not so with Judas Iscariot. Luke says, "Satan entered into Judas called Iscariot, who was of the number of the twelve; he went away and conferred with the chief priests and officers how he might betray him to them" (Luke 22:3–4). Even with the twelve disciples Jesus chose, both Jesus and Satan stood at the door of their hearts in crucial decisions. According to their and our choice, only one becomes incarnate in us as the one whom we will serve. But we ourselves open the door and let in one or the other.

The Character of Satan

The biblical story fleshes out the personification of temptation in Satan. It describes vividly the character of Satan somewhat as follows.

Satan is, even in the description in Job, adversarial in nature. Satan appears as being "over against" both God and human beings. The rawest statement of the devil's adversarial character is found in Revelation 2:10: "Behold, the devil is about to throw some of you into prison, that you may be tested, and for ten days you will have tribulation." The antithesis is in Jesus' victorious exultation when the seventy whom he had sent out returned and said, "Lord, even the demons are subject to us in your name!" Then Jesus said, "I saw Satan fall like lightning from heaven" (Luke 10:17–18). In apocalyptic interpretations of the Gospel, Satan is not just adversarial; Satan is engaged in warfare against the living Christ in heaven and on earth.

Satan's basic character, however, is that of the father of lies. Jesus says of the devil, "He . . . has nothing to do with the truth, because there is no truth in him. When he lies, he speaks according to his own nature, for he is a liar and the father of lies" (John 8:44). Deception, self-deception, pretense, guile, subterfuge, gamesmanship—these are the stock-in-trade of the great pretender, the father of lies. This central nature of the personification of temptation provides a starting point for a more empirical study of the psychological mechanisms of temptation.

A Biblical Psychology
of the Personification of Temptation

In all fairness, I must say I believe that no honest reading of the counsel of God in the scriptures can omit or even be casual about the reality of evil in both the being and the personification of Satan. However, the whole counsel of God goes further than presenting Satan as the ultimate source of all evil. To the contrary, the scripture just as often attributes evil to conflict in the human psyche in which our own human desires lure us into bondage to finite, creaturely, deceptive objects of our ultimate loyalty. This might be identified as a distinctly religious psychology of temptation, wherein the struggle is not between God and us, with Satan as an excuse, an object on which to project our responsibility, but between God and ourselves as to whether we shall love God and our neighbor as ourselves or whether we will deceive ourselves and become idolaters of the objects of our desires. Therefore, let us hold firmly to our faith in God and search out an empirical explanation of the mechanisms of temptation in the divine/human encounter that faithfully reflects all the teachings of the New Testament.

A faith statement about a given phenomenon or event in human experience focuses ordinarily on the "thatness" or existence of the phenomenon. A faith statement can absorb mystery and reveal in awe the evidence of things hoped for and the unknownness of things not seen. A scientific statement about the same phenomenon or event is not satisfied with the "thatness" but probes the mystery for an empirical explanation of the process of the phenomenon. A scientific statement is thus concerned with the "howness," the mechanism of the event. If it is indeed spontaneous and miraculous, the scientific spirit is concerned with how the event can be reproduced or caused to happen again.

Remarkably enough, in the biblical story, we find both of these concerns, not just one. The Wisdom literature is filled with empirical descriptions of the "howness" of life. When it comes to the phenomenon of the personification of temptation, the apostles Paul and James seem to be the most adept at describing the "how" of the human struggle of the soul in temptation. The two most vivid accounts are found in Romans 1:19–20 and James 1:12–15.

Romans 1:19–20

Paul clearly identifies the realm of natural phenomena in the created order. He says that "ever since the creation of the world [God's] invisible nature, namely, his eternal power and deity, has been clearly perceived in the things that have been made" (Rom. 1:20). He goes on to describe how human beings have lived and acted contrary to the ways in which they have been created.

We could take contemporary examples. The human lungs were not made to be contaminated with tobacco and marijuana. The human sexual organs were not made to be used in degrading forms of sexual behavior or promiscuously with multiple partners. The human body was not made to absorb continuous large quantities of alcohol, cocaine, crack, or other drugs. When one health official was asked how the mounting costs of health care in this country could be reduced, she replied that using tobacco, marijuana, and alcohol, drunken driving, drug addiction, and promiscuous sex cause increased medical costs. One estimate suggests that by 1992 we will have 300,000 children with birth defects as a result of the use of drugs by mothers during pregnancy! The cost of caring for even one of these children is astronomical.

Paul speaks clearly when he says that people have dishonored their bodies among themselves because "they exchanged the truth about God for a lie and worshiped and served the creature rather than the Creator" (Rom. 1:25).

This, then, is the mechanism, the "how," of the personification of temptation that leads to sin. The central name of that sin is idolatry. The commitment to lies carries with it self-deception and all the psychological mechanisms of self-defense—projection, fantasy formation, reaction formation, displacement, undoing, and many more.

Idolatry—worshiping the creature rather than the Creator—and lies—exchanging the truth of God for a lie—somewhere lurking in the background is the tempter, the father of lies. Paul definitely believed that Satan was the great deceiver and active in the world (Rom. 16:20; 1 Cor. 5:5; 7:5; 2 Cor. 2:11; 11:14; 2 Thess. 2:9). However, in this passage in Romans he makes no reference to Satan. He focuses on the individual's or group's deceptive exchange of the truth of God for a lie and the self-chosen worship of the creature rather than the worship of the Creator. The end result is idolatry of that part of creation to which a person attaches himself or herself.

These idolatrous attachments produce compulsive obsessions of many kinds. A person becomes possessed by that which he or she has allowed to hook them, such as idolizing work or marriage. That object to which or to whom they attach themselves for all practical purposes becomes their god. Their lives are centered around this object or person. Their existence lives and moves and has its being in terms of this attachment. In psychological terms, they become obsessed and compulsively attached to a person, a behavior, or a substance to which they are devoted and which has become their ultimate concern. As you can readily see, this is not just a psychological or psychiatric assessment. It includes the Tillichian definition of the demonic. Paul Tillich insisted throughout his work that for us to place anything finite, created, or proximate at the center of our ultimate concern is idolatry. To do so is to become possessed by the demonic. He says in *Systematic Theology* (I, p. 114), "The demonic blinds, it does not reveal. In the state of demonic possession, the mind is not really 'beside itself,' but rather it is in the power of elements of itself which aspire to be the whole mind which grasp the center of the rational self and destroy it." This is a phenomenology of the way in which "the god of this world" first enters the center of our decision-making freedom, enchants us with lies, beguiles the mind, even through pious religiosity, and finally does a corporate takeover of our lives. In the form of our obsession we become possessed and lose our freedom of decision making. We fall down and worship that which is no god.

Even the most piously religious person can be entrapped in the legalism of his or her faith, as Paul eloquently confesses in Romans 7 or—to the Galatians—expresses his concern that they were "in bondage to beings that by nature are no gods." They were turning back again "to the weak and beggarly elemental spirits, whose slaves you want to be once more." He admonished them: "For freedom Christ has set us free; stand fast therefore, and do not submit again to a yoke of slavery" (Gal. 4:8, 9; 5:1).

When, therefore, we speak of being possessed by demons, Paul describes the process without reference to external beings entering the human person. We are possessed by our self-deceiving choice of a no god, an idol whereby we have exchanged the worship of the Creator for the worship of the creature. As Wordsworth says:

> The world is too much with us; late and soon,
> Getting and spending, we lay waste our powers:
> . . . .
> We have given our hearts away, a sordid boon!

James 1:13–15

The second psychological description of the process of temptation in the New Testament is somewhat different. I have already given the quotation in chapter 1, but I come back to it here for emphasis. Whereas some blame their temptation on Satan, others blame their temptation on God. In a pragmatic, no-nonsense way, the author of James says:

Let no one say when he [or she] is tempted, "I am tempted by God"; for God cannot be tempted with evil and he himself tempts no one; but each person is tempted when he [or she] is lured and enticed by his [or her] own desire. Then desire when it has conceived gives birth to sin; and sin when it is full-grown brings forth death.

Gerald May writes in *Addiction and Grace* (p. 1) that "after twenty years of listening to the yearnings of people's hearts, I am convinced that all human beings have an inborn desire for God." Augustine presents a less optimistic view of the human heart in his opening prayer of *The Confessions:* "And man, who is part of your creation, wishes to praise you. You arouse him to take joy in praising you, for you have made us for yourself, and our heart is restless until it rests in you." Augustine seems to modify the inbornness of our desire to praise God with an additional inbornness, our restlessness of heart. He says we carry about in us our mortality and our testimony to our sin and testimony that God resists the proud. The desire of which James speaks seems to me to be the desire that is made restless by our mortality, our pride, and our desire to see if we cannot improve on God by creating a god of our own or, more likely, by trying to be or replace God.

Yet, as May points out, with the image of God very much alive in all of us, the proud desire to surpass God is not a wholehearted one. We remain, as Augustine says, restless. This restlessness is our ambivalence, our lack of wholeheartedness. Hence our freedom is not complete. Working against it is the powerful force of compulsive obsession. Psychologically, the obsession uses up energy. It is like a psychic malignancy sucking our life force into specific obsessions and compulsions, leaving less and less for other people and other pursuits. "Spiritually, addiction is a deep-seated form of idolatry. The objects of our addiction become our false gods. These are what we worship, what we attend to, where we give our time and energy, *instead of love*" (p. 13).

Special Temptations

Clinical experience in caring for persons, enhanced by careful spiritual reflection on my own temptations, reveals examples of specific temptations to obsession, seen psychologically, or to idolatry, seen spiritually.

Marriage as the Chief End of Life

The institution of marriage is an earthly institution. As Jesus said, "Those who are accounted worthy to attain to that age and to the resurrection from the dead neither marry nor are given in marriage" (Luke 20:35). However, regardless of how fragile the institution of marriage is, many look upon it as the chief end of their existence. The Presbyterian catechism opens with the question: "What is the chief end of [a person]?" The answer is: "To glorify God, and to enjoy [God] forever." Clinically, we see just the opposite, and if we plumb our own values to the depths, we see just the opposite too. Our whole existence and serenity often depend directly on the state of our marriage and family.

I conferred with a hospital patient several years ago who was profoundly, suicidally depressed. She said that if her husband ever divorced her, she would kill herself. She had begun psychiatric treatment with a very skillful physician and seemed to have improved. However, a few weeks later she decided that her husband was indeed going to end the marriage. For seventeen years she had repeatedly threatened suicide. On this occasion she did not just threaten, she took her own life. Her addictive dependence on being married to her husband destroyed all chances of freedom for either one of them to enjoy other pursuits.

The opposite of this tragedy is the insight of President Ellis Fuller of the Southern Baptist Theological Seminary. At a faculty-staff dinner he introduced his wife, Elizabeth, by saying, "I want to present to you the most dangerous person in my life, my wife. She is most dangerous because she is Christ's nearest rival for first place in my life."

Chronic Rage and Self-Deception Between Divorced Spouses

One of the fantasies that fills the imaginations of persons seeking divorce is that the legal act of divorce will cause the despised spouse to disappear completely from their lives. They imagine that divorce will simply vaporize the other person. After the divorce they are brought back to reality. Legal entanglements such as deciding on the support and supervision of children merely shift the battleground of their war with each other. As one former wife expressed it, "My divorced husband no longer lives in our house, but through the children he says and does things that make me so angry that he lives in my head rent-free, dominating all my thoughts and actions. This has got to stop, and I am the only person who can do it."

Thank God she did not have to do it in isolation. She had a strong support system of friends and a faithful and competent pastoral counselor, even though she was alienated from her church because of being divorced. The overpowering force of a desire for control, the need for revenge, and the settled aversion between divorced partners, especially where there are young children, can become a devastating obsession, an idolatry in its own right.

The opposite kind of fantasy of divorced persons is that they will remain close friends. The pursuit of this fantasy may be filled with self-deception, confusion, and petty gamesmanship. A more realistic goal would be to establish a civil and diplomatic relationship based upon recognizing the divorced spouse as a human being made in the image of God and for whom Christ died. The divorce decree is a social contract in which the "party of the first part" and the "party of the second part" accept specific responsibilities. It is like a treaty. Its stipulations are scrupulously kept, and the war is over.

To recognize the warfare as a struggle to be a "winner" in the rivalry over a spouse or a son or daughter is an active deterrent to addiction to and idolatry of one or all of them. It is the core psychological and spiritual component in the much-used concept of "co-dependence." We owe it to each other as spouses, parents, and sons and daughters to discipline each other with the kind of wisdom Ellis Fuller displayed. Errant sons or daughters, fathers or mothers, caught in the clutches of alcoholism or drug addiction, deserve all the care we can give them when they are helpless—as they occasionally become—or when they are being dealt with unjustly by lawyers, the police, or an alienated spouse. But we cannot with safety to them or to ourselves try to become their redeemer and salvation. They are busy trying to be their own gods. Such efforts on our part makes us their competitor in enabling their addiction with an addiction of our own—to be their sole salvation. We both have to come to the first conclusion of the Twelve Steps of Alcoholics Anonymous: "We admitted that we were powerless over alcohol—that our lives had become unmanageable." Then we take the second step: "We came to believe that a Power greater than ourselves could restore us to sanity."

Institutional Idolatry

In the work world, we move from the primary institution of the home to the secondary institution of the place where we make our living. The company, the university, or the government agency alluringly and easily become our ultimate concern, our raison d'être, the be-all and end-all of our existence. We overinvest our being in these institutions. If indeed a new coalition of power takes over and a perestroika destabilizes the comfortable niche we have carved out for ourselves, our whole lives are thrown into pandemonium. In institutional restructuring, a vast amount of grief due to changes made is normal. However, for some the temptation is great to make this grief, filled with bitterness as it regularly is, a continuing way of life. If we choose to personify this evil by conducting a continuing grudge war with the institution, by allowing our thought, conversation, and behavior to be shaped by the trauma of being pushed out, we have begun an addiction and made an idol of the institution.

George F. Kennan, the wise old man of United States foreign policy, was ambassador to Moscow and, earlier in his life, a holder of many significant positions representing the U.S. government in the period before, during, and immediately after World War II. But in a change-of-administrations shuffle, he was relieved of his diplomatic post. In *Sketches from a Life* (p. 173), he seemed to feel that life was over: "My day is past . . . I am . . . an anachronism . . . I, too, have been passed by and do really mind too much—because the present is uninteresting."

Kennan was only fifty-two years of age when he wrote these words! However, he broke through the normal grief that was prompted by radical change. He rebuilt his life around several new foci of interest and by all estimates made his greatest contribution to life *after* the loss of his government position. He withstood the temptation to give in to grief. His other alternative would have been to make this loss the center of his existence and become addicted to his idolatry of the State Department. Instead, he became a beloved senior statesman whose opinion was eagerly sought and respected.

These are two illustrations of how persons are "lured and enticed" by their own desires. The possibilities are deadly. If they yield when being tempted by their own desire, the desire conceives destructive thoughts, fantasies, and actions. When they are full grown they bring forth death. In some cases, this is not a metaphorical use of the term. It is literally the end of life.

The object to which a person is idolatrously attached—be it a substance, a sexual habit, a chronic hate match between two people, an institutional controversy, or a job problem—personifies temptation. Only the providence of God provided on a day-by-day basis is sufficient to break the attachment to such objects. As the hymn "Jesus Calls Us O'er the Tumult" puts it:

> Jesus calls us from the worship
> Of the vain world's golden store,
> From each idol that would keep us,
> Saying, "Christian, love me more."

4

The Community
of Persecution

As we continue to probe the meaning of temptation in the human condition, we are suddenly ambushed by a realization that the psychological perspective of temptation is insufficient to explain in a modern idiom the largest form of temptation found in the Bible, especially in the New Testament, which stems from persecution. Individual devotionalism and psychotherapy will take us a small distance toward this understanding, and we will walk that distance with them.

However, as we shall see, the average middle-class Christian is unconscious of the relationships of temptation and persecution. We have an underclass of dispossessed, oppressed, tempted-to-violence people in the United States, of whom we repress most if not all of our awareness. Continents of spiritual territory lie between us and people who live no more than five to fifteen geographical miles away. More than this, people in such places as Central America, Eastern Europe, Afghanistan, Iran, and China have been and are being put to the test for their religious faith. Vaclav Havel, leader of the revolution in Czechoslovakia, says in his play *Temptation* (p. 33) that "modern man has repressed everything that might allow him to transcend himself. . . . He has crowned himself as the highest authority, so he can then observe with horror how the world is going to the dogs under that authority!" Havel speaks of the principalities, the powers, the world rulers of this present darkness (of whom Paul speaks in Ephesians 6:12) when he says in *Letters to Olga* (p. 320):

> The alien world into which we are thrown beckons to us and tempts us. . . . We are constantly being exposed to the temptation to stop asking questions and adapt ourselves to the world as it presents itself to us, to sink into it, to forget ourselves, to lie our way out of ourselves and our "otherness" and thus to simplify our existence-in-the-world.

This chapter will view temptation and persecution from two angles. First we will look at their individual and interpersonal dimensions as reflected in middle-class American church life. Second, we will look at the revolutionary dimensions of the church under oppression. Where the individual psychological approach does not suffice, these stories of prophetic spirits and of the church in revolt against oppression will give a much more adequate understanding of temptation. The African-American churches of this country in the struggle for civil rights, the Catholic church in Poland and Central America, and the Protestant churches in Romania all represent a corporate personality resisting the temptation to remain silent and conform to the ways of oppressors.

The New English Bible translates Matthew 6:12 as: "Do not bring us to the test, but save us from the evil one." Following the paradigm of the meanings of temptation, temptation under persecution would be a more catastrophic kind of testing than that of the passages of life in our developmental crises. Temptation in the face of persecution is the temptation to recant one's beliefs, to resort to violence against one's persecutors, or, if possible, just to disappear from the scene.

When we apply the biblical wisdom about persecution and temptation today, we must remember Jesus' words to his disciples as he came out of the garden of Gethsemane. He said, "Watch and pray that you may not enter into temptation; the spirit indeed is willing, but the flesh is weak" (Matt. 26:41; Mark 14:38). The contemporary American audience is asleep to the momentous persecutions of Christians and non-Christians alike going on in the world today. We are involved in the assumptions of success, prosperity, and the freedom to do as we please. We are not watching the possibilities that persecution might come to us. Our own country is on the brink of a chaotic revolution because of homelessness, poverty, drug addiction, and corruption in high places of government and finance. Therefore, when we apply the paradigm of meanings of temptation to persecution, we must say that we are apathetic, unaware, not watching, asleep to the peril at our door.

A Persecuted Community

Although we rarely think of temptation with persecution, the community of faith that wrote the New Testament was persecuted for its belief in Jesus Christ. It was a persecuted community. The word "temptation" or "test" often refers to the breaking point at which a tortured person recants his or her faith. Jesus' most specific description of the persecution in store for his disciples is found in Matthew 10:16–23:

> Behold, I send you forth as sheep in the midst of wolves; so be wise as serpents and innocent as doves. Beware of men; for they will deliver you up to councils, and flog you in their synagogues, and you will be dragged before governors and kings for my sake, to bear testimony before them and the Gentiles. When they deliver you up, do not be anxious how you are to speak or what you are to say; what you are to say will be given to you in that hour; for it is not you who speak, but the Spirit of your Father speaking through you. Brother will deliver up brother to death, and the father his child, and children will rise against parents and have them put to death; and you will be hated by all for my name's sake. But he who endures to the end will be saved. When they persecute you in one town, flee to the next; for truly, I say to you, you will not have gone through all the towns of Israel, before the Son of man comes.

An easily missed reference in this passage is that Jesus says that the occasion of the persecution would be when the disciples began to challenge the Jewish establishment and to extend the gospel to the Gentiles. (For further insight see T. W. Manson, *The Epistle to the Hebrews,* pp. 25–31.) The witnesses, or martyrs, were declaring that a new era had arrived, when the extension of the Gospel to the Gentiles would supersede the "most favored nation" concept of the Jews.

In the second place, this community of faith was both a community of persecution *and* an eschatological community of high expectation that the Lord Jesus Christ, crucified, buried, resurrected, and ascended into heaven, would return before the members had gone through all the towns of Israel. This expectation gave people courage and hope as they faced persecution. The worst thing that could befall this community was that its members would deny their faith and acquiesce in their persecutors' charges of blasphemy. This would be apostasy, the most heinous of sins against the Holy Spirit, for which the early Christians felt they would not be forgiven.

An example of this in action is the witness of Stephen, who was "full of grace and power [and] did great wonders and signs among the people" (Acts 6:8). Stephen's revolutionary teachings led to his persecution and death. His capacity to meet the test and not deny his faith in the Lord Jesus Christ made him the first Christian martyr. His steadfast belief in the "coming of the Son of man" enabled him to withstand the temptation to fall away and return to the tenets, practices, and customs of Judaism. He and other Christians were being persecuted. The worst sin they could commit would be to recant their faith in Jesus Christ. This was the great temptation.

Temptation and the Test of Faith

Let us look at this from a twentieth-century perspective. The story of Stephen has a far-away and long-ago ring for our middle-class affluent active church members. On the surface we can say, We are Christians. We enjoy much approval, status, and even prosperity by being Christians. Few of us are ever persecuted for our faith. We have no fear of having committed the unpardonable sin (although some of us appear in mental hospitals laden with this fear). We are free of the fear of being tested for our faith in Christ. Therefore, persecution is seen as an obsolete temptation.

However, let us take a closer look at our present-day religious life. The culture-ridden religious community today has abandoned Stephen's radical revolutionary stance and is no longer persecuted. In many instances, the customs and traditions of different faith groups have become encrusted. Instead of being persecuted, members of the Christian establishment have in specific instances become the persecutors! Their instruments of torture are psychological and social rather than physical and violent. Nevertheless, this is a refined form of torture. For example, a religious group may have a dry and hardened set of dogmas consisting of certain catchword slogans and a generous mixture of political obeisance to nationalistic political litmus tests for membership in their group. If members say "shibboleth" to these dogmas and catchwords, they are safe. If they hold contrary positions, their jobs in the religious bureaucracy are at risk and they are excluded by neglect or are harassed until they leave their place of service.

If young persons preparing for Christian ministry choose the "wrong" seminary and develop a different interpretation of scripture and Christian practice, their family and home church may ostracize them. They cannot go home again. A young woman who does this and dares to seek ordination as well may suffer even more persecution. For some, she has broken caste and class barriers as well as the rudiments of the faith!

A considerable number of my counselees have damaging psychological perceptions of themselves arising from a harsh, hostility-ridden religious upbringing. They perceive themselves as "bad," guilt-ridden, anxious and unsure of themselves. These feelings hinder their competence as parents and often make them obsessively perfectionistic in their jobs. They work their fingers to the bone, trying to win the acceptance and approval of their parents. Even when the parents are dead, their persecuting moralisms still live in the memory of their offspring.

How easy it is for members of a first generation of a persecuted religious minority to become third-, fourth-, fifth-, or thousandth-generation members who turn and become the persecutors! They inflict wounds that draw no blood but twist the spiritual growth of minds, especially young minds. These ostracized persons experience isolation from the grace of the Lord. Jesus Christ invites persons burdened with the curse of legalism to take up the yoke that is easy and the burden that is light in the midst of a fellowship of others who manifest that grace, affection, and profound acceptance. Sometimes these persons find such understanding in an individual teacher in a school of higher education. Sometimes they find it in a church of a different denomination. Sometimes they find it in an organization like Fundamentalists Anonymous. At other times they find grace and acceptance from a psychiatrist, maybe a highly educated Jewish physician with more compassion and understanding than the Christians they know! Or they will find this acceptance and grace in a self-help group such as Alcoholics Anonymous. And sometimes they "find grace to help in time of need" from a pastoral counselor who is ecumenically oriented and can help them find the strengths in their religious heritage while enabling them to reveal their hurts from this tradition at the same time, in order that the grace of the living presence of God may heal their wounds.

Temptation and Persecution
Beyond the Walls of the Church

The relation between temptation and persecution brings a social, cultural, and political context to our discussion. We cannot stick merely to individualistic, pietistic concerns and grasp the full significance of temptation and persecution. Purely psychological categories are inadequate. We must consider this topic in a sociocultural context. We cannot restrict our attention to such instances within the walls of the churches to grasp the largest and deepest meaning of temptation and persecution. Admittedly these are the kinds of cases of temptation and persecution about religious commitments we see in pastoral counseling. However, we need to lift our eyes to the masses of

people enduring persecution today in order to see this relation of temptation to persecution in the largest meanings of the New Testament. This involves great social movements and upheavals of our time and focal personalities in those movements.

The Nonviolence of Mahatma Gandhi

A major contemporary example of the interaction of temptation and persecution is Mohandas Karamchand Gandhi. He won the name Mahatma (great-souled) in India because of his political, social, and religious leadership.

Gandhi studied law in England but soon began to apply it to great social injustices. His first such use came when a company asked him to be their legal representative in South Africa. He went to Pretoria, but though traveling on a train with a first-class ticket as an English-dressed barrister he was nevertheless told to ride in a baggage car because he was a person of color. When he refused to do so, he was thrown off the train. As he shivered with cold throughout the night, he vowed to fight racial injustice in South Africa.

Gandhi spent twenty-one years (1893–1914) in perfecting the spiritual and political principle of action he called "satyagraha," or "truth force." He returned to India in 1915 and began applying this principle to labor disputes and India's struggle for independence. He wrote articles, he fasted in defiance of British rule, and conducted noncooperation campaigns. As L. D. Shinn writes in the *Abingdon Dictionary of Living Religions* (p. 272), Gandhi "asserted that true 'self rule' *(swarāj)* is first self-control and a disciplined will." The inner battle of temptation to violence must be won first; only then can one reach economic and political self-determination. "To act nonviolently is not merely to withhold angry actions from a superior foe . . . but to act with the force *[graha]* of truth *[satyā]* honed by compassion and self-restraint. For Gandhi the means is 'the ends in the making.' "

By his own account, Gandhi's remarkable character was in an important way shaped by Jesus' Sermon on the Mount. He took the ethic of Jesus into the social and political realm and applied it to the struggle against principalities and powers in high places. He effected the independence of his people without a gun, an army, or a military strategy. Yet at the center of his powerful life was a massive struggle of the soul to resist the temptation of hatred and violence. Shinn notes that, for Gandhi, "hatred is far more dangerous to the one who hates than to the one who is hated." Yet hatred ended Gandhi's life when a Hindu radical shot him to death. Persecution caused him to lead a life of self-discipline in an ordered resistance to the temptation to hate. The undisciplined fellow Hindu assassinated him, completing the worst that persecution could offer. Gandhi stood the test and kept the faith, but he lost his life at the hands of one who could not control his hatred.

Martin Luther King, Jr., and the Civil Rights Movement

Martin Luther King, Jr., was greatly influenced by Gandhi. He attended Morehouse College in Atlanta and Crozer Theological Seminary in Chester, Pennsylvania, and received a Ph.D. in Systematic Theology at Boston University. He said that before reading Gandhi he had thought the ethics of Jesus were applicable only in individual relationships. When he read Gandhi, he changed his mind.

Gandhi had lifted the love ethic of Jesus above action between individuals and applied it in large social conflicts. Love transformed society as well. Consequently, King formulated five principles of nonviolence: (1) Nonviolence does resist, it is not a coward's way; (2) nonviolence aims at giving understanding to an opponent, not destroying him or her; (3) nonviolence opposes forces of evil instead of persons; (4) the nonviolent person accepts suffering and does not strike back; and (5) nonviolent people also avoid "internal violence of the spirit" (King, *Stride Toward Freedom,* pp. 102–103). This "internal violence of the spirit" is the proving ground of temptation.

With this as his often repeated commitment, King began his ministry as pastor of Dexter Avenue Baptist Church in Montgomery, Alabama, in 1954. Within a year, Mrs. Rosa Parks was arrested and charged with violating the Montgomery city segregation code after refusing to give up her seat to a white man. King led a city-wide boycott of Montgomery buses in response. This began a long list of nonviolent protests over the South. As a result King was persecuted in many ways. In January 1956 a bomb was thrown into his home, though no one was hurt; King calmed and dispersed the angry mob that gathered. Finally a U.S. District Court and the U.S. Supreme Court declared the segregation of city buses unconstitutional and the buses were desegregated in December 1956.

King was repeatedly arrested and jailed on such charges as loitering, perjury on income tax returns—for which he was acquitted—trespassing, violating probation in a traffic charge, obstructing a sidewalk, disorderly conduct, and being an "unwanted guest" in Florida. He was stoned in Chicago. Finally, on April 4, 1968, he was shot in the neck by a sniper in Memphis and died later at St. Joseph's Hospital. As with Gandhi, an assassin's bullet ended his life. James Earl Ray was later convicted for the murder. (See "The Living King," *Ebony,* January 1986, pp. 36–108.)

King was not the sole speaker for black people in the civil rights movement. In July 1966, Stokely Carmichael's "black power" concept which described a militant, actively aggressive approach to ending racial injustice, was endorsed by the Congress of Racial Equality and its new director, Floyd McKissick. However, primarily because of King's emphasis on voter registration, which has been taken up by Jesse Jackson and others, the civil rights and black power movements moved into the active political process at the balloting stations. In the fall of 1989, a black governor was elected in the state of Virginia and a black mayor was elected in the city of New York.

The discipline of Martin Luther King, Jr., for which he paid with his life, has only begun to realize the fruits of racial peace and creativity. His struggle with the temptations of rage, hatred, and violence is another example of the way in which temptation and persecution are interwoven.

László Tökés of Romania

Another living human document has come to light in the struggle of the Romanian people's revolt in January of 1990 against the draconian rule of Nicolae Ceausescu. The people had severe shortages of such everyday basics as food and fuel. They were harassed and tyrannized by the Securitate, the security police.

Rising up against this, Pastor László Tökés protested against the regime. In response he was denied rationing cards; the security police broke into his apartment and stabbed him. Two friends helped him fight them off. He was deported from his parish in Timisoara to a very small village, Minei. "When police deported him to this small village . . . a peaceful vigil outside his church erupted into an anti-regime riot. The demonstrations soon spread throughout the country, finally toppling dictator Nicolae Ceausescu" *(Christian Science Monitor,* January 25, 1990, p. 14).

Pastor Tökés is presumably not committed to a specifically nonviolent discipline. Yet it is equally apparent that neither he nor his followers engaged in armed resistance. Many of them were killed; estimates range from a few hundreds to many thousands. In any event, this is another case of the power of self-control and resistance to the temptations of violence in the face of persecution.

Nelson Mandela of South Africa

Nelson Mandela in South Africa is another example of being tested in the wake of persecution. Jailed for twenty-seven years, he stood the test to which he was put for his leadership of ongoing resistance to apartheid, the systematic exclusion of blacks from the mainstream of the social, economic, and political life of South Africa.

Mandela is the spiritual leader of the African National Congress, which was an outlawed organization until a history-making pronouncement of President de Klerk gave them recognition to negotiate for blacks. Its leaders were either in prison or in exile in other countries.

Gandhi's ideal of nonviolence is a part of the ANC's commitment, with one reservation: to fight back in self-defense against white violence. Mandela has now been released from prison. In a policy-making speech to hundreds of thousands at a soccer stadium, he defined the essence of the temptation, the test, to which he and his people are being put. He urged them to maintain self-discipline and give the white leadership no occasion for violence against them. They are to go to negotiating tables with the white leadership, not to violence in the streets.

This is the crucible of temptation in which Mandela and South African blacks find themselves at this time. No one knows what the results will be. Nevertheless, here again are other instances of the persecution and turbulent social and cultural upheavals that puts leaders like Gandhi, King, Tökés, Mandela, and many others to the test. The critical, rarely spoken issue is whether Mandela will be allowed to live in order to lead. Will he too be assassinated, after twenty-seven years in prison? To this threat he responds, "I have fought against white domination and black domination. I have cherished the ideal of a democratic and free society. It is an ideal for which I am prepared to die" (*Christian Science Monitor,* February 16, 1990, p. 1).

Vaclav Havel

Another struggler with the repression of tyrannical regimes is Vaclav Havel, the new president of Czechoslovakia, who once wrote plays and letters that were critical of the Communist regime. While in prison the first time, he was able to write a petition to the Public Prosecutor with just enough ambiguity to win his release. When he succeeded in this way, he berated himself in *Letters to Olga* (p. 351) for having yielded to the temptation of cleverness.

> It's not hard to stand behind one's successes. But to accept responsibility for one's failures . . . that is devilishly hard! But only then does the road lead . . . to a radically new insight into the mysterious gravity of my existence as an uncertain enterprise and to its transcendental meaning. . . . I have my failure to thank for the fact that for the first time in my life I stood directly in the study of the Lord God himself.

In his play *Temptation,* Havel describes an Institute of Science dedicated to producing a "science" that fitted the propaganda purposes of the government regime personified in the Director, a sort of prototype of Satan. Foustka, the leading character, begins to pursue this kind of science to its ultimate extreme in the study of the occult. He is visited by a tempter of a mentor, Fistula. Fistula's slippery logic appeals to Foustka so much, they form a pact to work together. The whole scheme falls apart when the Director confronts Foustka with the fact that the mentor, Fistula, is the Director's employee and spy.

The play moves into deeper and deeper layers of surreal use of the "rational" into the irrational for a conclusion in which all the scientists gather in a "witches' garden." Only a Czechoslovakian audience can fathom the depths of the lies and distortions of the agency established to ferret out the "irrational tendencies" of the populace. The play is a finely honed dissection of the conditions of the modern bureaucracy. Havel reminds us that bureaucratic deception is universal. He says (p. 86): "To deceive a liar is fine, to deceive a truth teller is allowable, but to deceive the very instrument that gives us the strength to deceive and that allows you to advance to deceive with impunity—that, you truly cannot expect to get away with!"

This Faustian play is a vehicle of protest, like many of the writings that got Havel in prison. His most intense description of people in temptation is in *Letters to Olga* (p. 375): "Yes, man is in fact nailed down—like Christ on the Cross—to a grid of paradoxes. . . . He balances the torment of not knowing his mission and the joy of carrying it out, between nothingness and meaningfulness. And, like Christ, he is in fact victorious by virtue of his defeats."

The prayer not to be put to the test of persecution continues

to be prayed by the spiritual beneficiaries of the heritage of
Stephen. People like the six Catholic priests in El Salvador,
who were executed with their housekeeper, follow in Stephen's
tradition as well.

To many who consider temptation to be a private, personal
experience, this roll call of persons involved in massive revolu-
tions against principalities and powers may seem to be going
afield from our topic. However, this assumption reflects something of the insulation of both the ecclesiastical and the psychotherapeutic communities from these world-shaking tests of
human personalities in the crucible of temptation.

We are akin to the disciples who were asleep outside the
garden of Gethsemane while Jesus was undergoing the agony of
accepting or letting the cup of his crucifixion pass. He had
asked the sons of Zebedee if they could drink of the cup that he
was about to drink. They had said, "We are able." He had told
them they would indeed drink his cup (Matt. 20:22–23). But
they were asleep to the possibility at Gethsemane. We too are
numb with apathy and asleep to the reality of persecution for
our faith. We slumber while people in our own city drink of the
cup of his crucifixion in our violent world. We are like what
Douglas John Hall calls, in *Lighten Our Darkness,* "the offi-
cially optimistic society" (pp. 43ff.). This, he says (pp. 99–100),
grows out of

> the whole intention of modern Christianity . . . to rid itself al-
> together of the doctrine of sin. It is an embarrassment. . . . But sin
> was reduced to something domestic. It became synonymous with
> immorality. "Sin" became "sins." Thus the churches could con-
> tinue in their role as "curer of souls" without entering into the
> social and political fabric of life as questioner of basic cultural
> assumptions.

To consider sins as a list of personal offenses obscures the
reality of sin as a universally human condition affecting masses
of people. Such deletion of the reality of sin can be seen as a
broad and deep social-psychological phenomenon of repression. Long before Freud explained repression as an individual
experience of an unenlightened superego, repression was defined as the control of the masses by putting down by force
every vestige of opposition to an oppressive ruling regime's
policies. Today, psychiatrists like Robert Coles and Robert Lifton have devoted much of their research and writing to this
kind of repression. Coles has done full studies of racial minori-
ties; migrant workers, sharecroppers, and mountaineers; and
privileged children and young people, recording what they

have to say about their life situations. (See *Children of Crisis; Migrants, Sharecroppers, Mountaineers; The South Goes North; Privileged Ones.*) In *The Broken Connection,* Lifton writes about the break between the "optimistic society" of which Hall speaks and the seething anger, rage, and violence of people like Vietnam veterans. Cole's and Lifton's works depict a whole new universe of human beings under subtle persecution and temptation. This universe is a far cry from the domestication of both church life and psychotherapeutic practices today.

Is Persecution Deserved, Real, or Imagined?

Temptation comes through persecution at a highly individual level or through involvement in a large social struggle with persecutors. Both the New Testament and psychotherapy ask whether persecution is deserved, real, or imagined. Spiritual discernment is required to distinguish the difference.

The knee-jerk reaction of persons who have done grossly antisocial acts or even petty acts of injustice is to accuse others of setting them up, plotting against them, or hounding them to death. In their own eyes they are victims, being persecuted by others. Essentially, though, they deserve the punishment they get.

On the contrary, as we have seen in the cases of Gandhi, King, Tökés, and Mandela, persecution is real, tangible, witnessed by the whole world. Many less-famous persons also suffer real persecution. Many are indeed hounded by sadistic employers, religious zealots, or law-enforcement officials. They are prone to feel that the whole world is against them.

Then there are the delusional paranoid persons, who imagine that they are being persecuted. They have bizarre delusions that mighty forces are conspiring to undo them. Yet in listening to their stories, there is often a grain of truth abiding in their paranoia: someone may have lied to them, for example, in order to get them into a hospital. Their self-deception is matched by real deception of others.

Harry Stack Sullivan, an eminent psychiatrist, had a useful concept for dealing with this threefold confusion of the deserved, the real, and the imagined persecution. He called it "consensual validation," whereby a person tests his or her perception by conferring with a community of trusted persons. This "testing of the spirits," by sharing our fears of persecution with others, helps keep us in touch with reality. The whole process of testing the reality and unreality of our feelings of being persecuted is a struggle with temptation itself to believe, move, and act upon a false or imagined assumption.

This process of testing the reality of persecution is where both biblical truth and psychological analysis converge. First John 4:1 states it best: "Beloved, do not believe every spirit, but test the spirits to see whether they are of God; for many false prophets have gone out into the world."

5

Temptation and Contemporary Psychological States

The main thrust of the preceding chapters has been toward a biblical psychology of temptation. This chapter will identify several contemporary psychological phenomena to provide a behavioral-science understanding of temptation. It has been said that today's most commonly shared idiom is psychological language. This is not just a contrasting of semantics. To the contrary, it is a cultural shift of idioms that are shared universally. The biblical idiom is foundational to the English language, especially the language found in the King James Version of the Bible, Chaucer's *Canterbury Tales,* and Shakespeare's plays. Not only are these works great literature; they largely defined the common speech of English-speaking persons. With the increased secularization of society, especially in America where it has been ruled unconstitutional to include Bible readings in the public schools, the biblical idiom has become strange to the tongues of even theological students. With the appearance of the Bible in more than twenty different translations and the demise of memorizing the Bible, the biblical idiom is less and less used in everyday speech (see Daniel J. Boorstin, *The Discoverers*). According to McCrum, Cran, and MacNeil's *The Story of English* (p. 113), "The King James Bible was published in the year Shakespeare began work on his last play, *The Tempest.* Both the play and the Bible are masterpieces of English, but there is one crucial difference between them. Whereas Shakespeare ransacked the lexicon, the King James Bible employs a bare 8000 words—God's teaching in homely English for everyman." Those eight thousand words remained the common idiom of English and American speech until this century. Gradually psychology and psychiatry secularized the language about temptation, although the language they created has a strong latent ethical content. An earlier generation would have said that "a spirit of rage" or uncleanness or fear or the like possessed a person. In this generation, we say they "have a problem."

Therefore, it is necessary here to connect with the readers of today by translating the biblical idiom into a more commonly known one, the psychological idiom. A lifelong dedication to this kind of translation will make it easy. Please note, however, that we are not simply translating one kind of English into another. We are building a bridge between theological and biblical works and psychodynamics. This is important, because the ultimate concerns of people are amputated from their consciousness if they have *only* a psychodynamic view of life. If we are cut loose from our awareness of our companionship with the Eternal, we are left to our own devices and become absorbed in our cosmic loneliness.

Furthermore, psychodynamic formulations are usually based on the assumption that the theorist is "objective" and "ethically" neutral. However, ethical issues and value judgments are cryptically present in these formulations. The biblical theological translation moves these cryptic value judgments into an articulate framework. The content of those ethical issues has been explicitly stated in the previous chapters on temptation. For example, the psychodynamic formulation of narcissism, when explicitly stated in biblical and ethical terms, is self-elevation, or hubris; the psychological concept of addiction is biblically akin to idolatry; and so on.

Approach-Avoidance Behavior

Approach-avoidance behavior occurs when the inner desires of a person conflict with each other. It is the result of opposing drives to do something and to refrain from doing something. Kaplan and Sadock (p. 1717) illustrate this as an explanation of stuttering. The person wants to say something and does not want to say it. The behavior is an expression of ambivalence, which means the coexistence of contradictory emotions, attitudes, values, or ideas.

For example, a man looks at the family automobile, which is paid for, and is happy with it. Then the new models come out. He listens to the television ads, reads the newspapers, and looks up the book value of the car, but he decides to keep it; it runs well, is paid for, and has no rust. However, on a day off, he wanders into the display room of a car dealer and considers how nice a new car would be. It *smells* so much better than the old one. But to buy it means committing to three, four, or five years of monthly payments. He decides again that "old is better." Once again he has resisted sales appeals and his own tempting desires.

However, the man then discusses the whole matter with his wife and children. They are excited and eager to get a new car. They enthusiastically grant permission, thereby tipping the scales of the approach-avoidance hassle, and the whole family goes out and buys a new car. Now the other side of the husband's ambivalence takes hold. Once the deal is made, he can easily justify having traded cars in more ways than can be counted. The approach-avoidance behavior is over.

A more tortured approach-avoidance pattern is characteristic of persons with damaging habits. They are double-minded about these actions. They both move toward them and are repelled by them. They halt between two opinions, to quote Elijah (1 Kings 18:21, KJV). For example, a student has formed bad study habits and persistently delays, never getting work done on time, often asking for extensions of time or incompletes on courses. The student approaches the task of the assignment and then backs off from it. This is a habit.

A habit may be either maladaptive, such as the procrastination of the student, or it may be constructive, relieving our conscious attention to do more attention-demanding tasks. An example would be the habit of fastening seat belts. The element of temptation enters when we persistently and even intentionally are tempted to ignore using seat belts at all.

When it comes to harmful habits, they can be replaced by new, constructive ones. Classic examples are smoking, drinking, drug use, gambling, and destructive sexual activity. An early conventional wisdom is that of William James, who gave guidelines for breaking old habits and forming constructive new ones. In *Talks to Teachers* (pp. 31–45), he gave five laws, which speak volumes about the dynamics of approach-avoidance behavior:

1: The acquisition of a new habit, or the leaving of an old one, requires that we must take care to launch ourselves with as strong and decided an initiative as possible.

2: Never suffer an exception to occur until the new habit is securely rooted in your life.

3: Seize the very first possible opportunity to act on every resolution you make, and on every emotional prompting you may experience in the direction of the habits you aspire to gain.

4: Don't preach too much . . . about habits or abound in good talk in the abstract. [This affirms Freud's comment that talk reduces the tendency to act.]

5:   Keep the faculty of effort alive in you by a little gratuitous exercise [of the habit] every day.

Addiction

A second psychological concept that is highly relevant to our study of temptation is addiction. Addiction can be viewed in several ways. It can be seen specifically to apply to obesity, dependence on alcohol or other drugs, uncontrolled gambling, and similar problems. Or addiction can be seen as a metaphor for other behaviors or temptations, such as repeatedly letting a spouse be physically abusive or depending inordinately on your work to relieve the anxieties and tensions of life. Then again, addiction can be seen as the compulsive need to help another addicted person beyond the point of common sense, reason, or ability. (This is commonly called co-dependency in psychological and drug rehabilitation literature.) Finally, addiction is increasingly being interpreted as characteristic of the whole human race in its tendency and persistence in forming idolatrous attachments.

This is the view of Gerald May, explained in *Addiction and Grace* (p. 13): "Spiritually addiction is a deep-seated form of idolatry. The objects of our addiction become our false gods. These are what we worship, what we attend to, where we give our time and energy, *instead of love.* Addiction, then, displaces and supplants God's love as the source and object of our deepest true desire . . . a counterfeit religious presence."

May considers addiction to apply to more than alcohol and drugs. Addiction can be to work, to a morbid love relationship, to a career, even to a religious system. He says (p. 97): "Addiction to a religious system, like addiction to anything else, brings slavery, not freedom. The structures of religion are meant to mediate God's self-revelation through community: they are not meant to be substitute gods." However, addiction to alcohol or drugs provides a working metaphor for all other kinds of addiction. It is a deceptive game with lethal power.

The Alcohol–Drug Abuse Game

Alcoholics and other drug addicts do not live in a social vacuum. They live in a family and community system that aids and abets their addiction. Eric Berne says in *Games People Play* (pp. 72–73) that the system's players make up a five-handed game of deceptive relationships: (1) The addict, who is the victim, or "it," to use Berne's term; (2) the Persecutor, usually played by a member of the opposite sex, probably a spouse; (3) the Rescuer, played by a therapist, a parent, or the paramour of an estranged spouse; (4) a Patsy or Dummy, the person who loans the addict money or hands out free food or lodging, without ever persecuting or trying to change him or her; and (5) the Connection, the supplier of the alcohol or the drugs. The Connection is a professional, says Berne; all the rest are amateurs.

Remarkably enough, the theme of persecution, the temptation to drink or use drugs, and the temptation of playing god as a rescuer all appear in this drama. In alcoholism, the Persecutor justifies (in another context this is a great theological word) the alcoholic in yielding to the temptation to drink. The Connection (commonly thought of as the tempter in biblical terms) provides the substance for the alcoholic. In an eerie way the "providence" of the Connection has replaced the providence of God. Thus on the human plane the game of alcoholism, filled with deception as it is, recapitulates the issues of faith in God—justification, providence, and the worship of the creature rather than the Creator.

Redemption for the addict lies in calling off the game. The victim ceases to blame the Persecutor and admits that life has become unmanageable. The victim needs to make a new connection with a greater Power and to look to that Power as the provider of strength day by day to withstand the temptation to drink or abuse drugs. The Rescuer needs to cease playing God, admit his or her helplessness, and call off the game of having all the answers. Then the Rescuer can invest confidence in the victim's own strength to bring sanity back into both their lives. Yet, having done this, the Rescuer needs to accept his or her frailty as a human being and become a fellow struggler with addiction along with the victim. Rescuers are also addicted—to "helping"—to such an extent that they must get daily fixes of helping or else anxiety will overwhelm them. They are unaware of the anger, resentment, and loss of self-esteem and self-worth that their helping engenders. They need to remember Oscar Wilde's oft-quoted comment: "I don't know why that man hates me. I never did anything to help him!"

Fantasy

If we think of temptation as the battle ground of character, fantasy is the ordnance department, providing ammunition for one side of the conflict. Fantasy is a product of the imagination. It can be a substitute for action, or it can be preparation or planning for later action. Fantasy may be conscious or unconscious, although these distinctions are not as useful, it seems to me, as asking whether the fantasy is close to reality or sealed off from reality. Fantasy that is close to reality might more accurately be called keen anticipation. Psychoanalyst Leo Spiegel says that fantasy as anticipation is forestalling "guilt-laden action." "Behind these issues shimmers the deep problem of the common roots of the responsibility for moral action and for self-observation" (p. 334). Fantasy that is sealed off from reality is thereby cut off from the ethical perceptions of the person and may break forth in irrational action. Thus testing of a fantasy against reality never happens.

In *Systematic Theology* (vol. 2, pp. 35–36), Paul Tillich relates fantasy to temptation in the following way: "Man experiences the anxiety of losing himself . . . by actualizing himself and his potentialities. He stands between the preservation of his dreaming innocence without experiencing the actuality of being and the loss of his innocence through knowledge, power, and guilt. The anxiety of this situation is the state of temptation."

Anxiety

Anxiety is the concept in the psychological repertoire that best encompasses what biblical theology calls temptation. Anxiety is a state arising from an awareness of what one wishes to do and a lack of the courage to do so. Yet the wish will not go away. It presents and re-presents itself, to be dealt with again and again in the debating rooms of the mind. Being anxious carries with it several bodily responses. One of these, a shortening of breath, is embedded in the roots of the word itself: the Latin word is *angere,* meaning "to choke in distress"; in Greek one word for anxiety is *stenochōreō,* meaning "to shorten the breath." However, other psychophysiological states also accompany anxiety, such as the painful awareness of being unable to do anything about a particular matter and a sense of impending and inevitable danger. A tense and physically exhausting alertness and vigilance, gastrointestinal and cardiovascular changes, and so on also accompany the state of anxiety.

When we relate these symptoms to temptation, they represent the halting state of indecision as to what to think, say, or do about a given situation. Obviously, the situation must be one that calls for a decision and a response. A person undergoes a struggle of the soul in a "valley of decision." Anxiety produces an extreme state of self-absorption that gets in the way of solving the problem in a realistic manner.

One can readily see that anxiety is different from fear in that it is more typically a reaction to unreal or imagined danger, whereas fear is a response to real danger or hazard. Anxiety can arise from the threat of losing control of one's emotions, particularly anger, or of doing what one would greatly like to do but is afraid to do because of the consequences. Anxiety attends maintaining a certain public image of oneself when in one's heart of hearts one would prefer to do otherwise.

Anxiety, furthermore, is related to the consequences or outcome of a given alternative that may be chosen. Kaplan and Sadock say (pp. 886–887): "The nature of the consequences that individuals fear determines the quality of anxiety they experience." Then they name four different qualities of anxiety. First is superego, or unenlightened conscience, anxiety, or the anxiety of prickings of conscience which arise when a person has done something that flouts his or her code of behavior. The critical anxiety is that the person will be found out. Second is separation anxiety, which a person experiences when he or she anticipates the leaving or loss of a loved one. Third is the fear of damage to one's own body, especially acute when it is the fear of damage or loss of one's genitals, commonly called castration anxiety. And fourth is impulse anxiety, or the panicky fear of losing control over one's impulses. A common fear is that a person will lose control over his or her rage.

Paul Tillich sees courage as the opposite of anxiety and its antidote. He explores anxiety deeply in his book *The Courage to Be,* speaking of courage as the self-affirmation of one's own being (p. 3). This theme is picked up by Heinz Kohut, a more recent psychoanalyst. He defines courage as "the ability to brave death and to tolerate destruction rather than to betray the nucleus of one's psychological being, that is, one's ideals" (*Self Psychology and the Humanities,* pp. 6–7). He continues in this essay on courage to identify the three characteristics of the courageous or heroic person: the presence of a fine sense of humor, the ability to respond to others with subtle empathy, and "generally at the time when the ultimate heroic decision has been reached and the agonizing consequences have to be faced, the suffusion of the personality with a profound sense of inner peace and serenity—a mental state akin to wisdom" (pp. 15–16).

Kohut describes the ethical imperative in the crisis of anxiety. He speaks in the idiom of psychology and psychoanalysis, but his strong ethical description of the heroic person is characteristic of the martyrs of the Christian faith, from Stephen to Dietrich Bonhoeffer. He inspires those of us in more mundane and less life-threatening situations of anxiety to take stock of our ideals and make a stand in their behalf. Only incidental to this is the way in which Kohut translates ethical imperatives that have been characteristic of living faith in God into a psychological idiom. One question remains, however: Where does this ethical resolve come from? Is it self-generated, by one's own efforts, or is it, as I assume, found in companionship with God's wisdom and presence?

Projection

Another psychological dynamic that describes temptation is projection. This dynamic is the unconscious mechanism by which a person attributes to other people those personal ideas, thoughts, and impulses that he or she finds undesirable or unacceptable.

Remarkably enough, the apostle Paul ferreted out the relation of faultfinding in another person to temptation in the faultfinder, saying that if a person "is overtaken in any trespass, you who are spiritual should restore him [or her] in a spirit of gentleness. Look to yourself, lest you too be tempted" (Gal. 6:1). I have held it to be axiomatic that the harsher a person is in condemning another person, the more likely he or she is to be struggling with the temptation to do the same thing or is already actually doing it.

Projection is the psychological mechanism most common in the paranoid personality disorder. Along with it is the delusion of grandeur that grows out of the person's sense of being "special," an exception to all rules, and superior to others in every way. A common religious phenomenon is that of a new convert in his or her redemption from an addiction, such as alcoholism or gambling. After becoming a Christian, this person becomes a zealot, insisting that everyone else in or out of the church have a similar religious experience. Such people see their old selves in everyone else. On the surface, it would seem that becoming intensely active in a religious organization after recently uniting with the group is a noble thing to do. However, as T. S. Eliot says, at the end of Part I of *Murder in the Cathedral:*

> The last temptation is the greatest treason:
> To do the right deed for the wrong reason.

Reaction Formation

Another strange expression of the unconscious struggles with temptation at the deepest layers of our being is the psychological dynamic of reaction formation. This is the unconscious management of tempting thoughts or behavior by expressing opposing thoughts or behaving in the opposite way. It is a negative expression of a given impulse, a "Mr. Clean" approach to the contaminating temptation. If a reaction formation represents a profound lasting instinctual conflict, such as a sexual conflict or a rage conflict, it can become an ongoing personality trait, usually an obsessive-compulsive personality disorder. In other words it becomes a way of life, not just a passing response to a transitory situation.

This dynamic of temptation is summarized by Shakespeare when Hamlet asks the queen what she thinks of the play within the play. She replies, "The lady doth protest too much, methinks" (III.ii.242). In religious behavior this dynamic once showed itself unexpectedly when I was standing in a shop door talking with a friend. Along the street came a very large man carrying a very large Bible under his arm and singing in a very loud voice a well-known gospel song. He passed by, and my friend commented, "I wonder what he was tempted to do or did last night!" He seemed to be protesting too much that he was religiously devout.

This appears also in the life of the church when an exceptionally active church member who advertises his business as the most honest place in town is one day indicted and later convicted for criminal business practices. Then the defenses collapse. As Shakespeare again says in *Hamlet* (IV.v.19–20):

> So full of artless jealousy is guilt
> It spills itself in fearing to be spilt.

Inner Conflict

A persistent psychodynamic theme among those that are relevant to our study of temptation is that of inner conflict. This theme goes all the way back to Socrates' prayer: "Give me beauty in the inner man and may the outward man and the inner man be the same." In the present era the transactional analysts of game theory have identified the patterns of deception that persist between the inner child of the past and the person struggling to be an adult in an adult world. Eric Berne originated this pattern of interpretation of our inner conflicts; see his *Transactional Analysis in Psychotherapy*.

A decade or two earlier, in a book that is still in print, Karen Horney, the founder of the American Institute of Psychoanalysis and a steadfast friend and colleague of theologian Paul Tillich, wrote descriptively and helpfully in her book *Our Inner Conflicts.* The basic inner conflict, Horney says (p. 335), is inconsistency:

> Inconsistencies are as definite an indication of the presence of conflicts as a rise in body temperature is of physical disturbance. To cite some common ones: A girl wants above all else to marry, yet shrinks from the advances of any man. A mother oversolicitous of her children frequently forgets their birthdays. A person always generous to others is stingy about small expenditures for himself. Another who longs for solitude never manages to be alone. Someone who is forgiving and tolerant toward most people is oversevere and demanding with himself."

Inconsistencies are grounded in the person's relationship to other people. Horney describes the interpersonal movement in three kinds of inner conflict.

Group One is made up of people who regularly *move toward other people.* They are compliant, with strong needs for approval and affection—so much so that they readily placate others to win their approval and affection. Horney says, "Where the patient errs is in claiming that all his frantic beating about for affection and approval is genuine, while in reality the genuine portion is heavily overshadowed by his insatiable urge to feel safe" (p. 51).

Group Two are those who *move against other people.* These people are aggressive and take "it for granted that everyone is hostile and refuses to admit that they are not. To him life is a struggle of all against all, and the devil take the hindmost" (p. 63).

Group Three are those who *move away from other people.* "What is crucial is their inner need to put emotional distance between themselves and others." They have a "striking need for self-sufficiency" (p. 75). In order to achieve self-sufficiency they must be extremely resourceful and clever as a way of compensating for their isolation. They even learn to get along without common needs in order to maintain their self-sufficiency.

The temptation common to all these persons is their struggle to avoid intimacy with other people and their inflexibility in relating to other people. They are tempted to demand that the whole world adjust to them. One common expression is, "Well, this is the way I am. Why can't you put up with me as I am?" Nor can they learn from others who are different from themselves. The basic temptation is hubris, or self-elevation, which is as old as the garden of Eden.

Common Themes in the Dynamics of Temptation

In this brief overview of some psychodynamics of temptation we see several common themes.

First, they all involve our capacity as human beings to deceive ourselves. This theme is also common in biblical and theological interpretations of temptation. In both accounts, the other person's faults are as plain as the nose on his or her face, but we cannot see *our* nose on *our* face.

Second, they all move on the assumption of the inner self as opposed to the outer self, as opposed to other people. Yet they all assume an interpersonal field of interacting selves. Temptations or inner conflicts arise out of this field of interpersonal relationships, not merely between the personal world and the material world. They are essentially social in nature.

Third, in none of these assessments of dynamics of inner conflict or temptation is there any discussion of the person's relationship to God. Here is the major difference between them and the biblical understanding and message concerning temptation.

William Sheehan and Jerome Kroll, in a study of 52 patients titled "Psychiatric Patients' Belief in General Health Factors and Sin as Causes of Illness," found that 23 percent believed that sin-related functions, such as sinful thoughts or acts, affected the development of their illnesses. They write (pp. 112–113): "Since humans appear constitutionally designed to seek meanings for the events of their lives, it is not surprising they will use a religious framework in this constant endeavor." Sheehan and Kroll encourage their colleagues to avoid glossing over the moral or transcendental importance of the disease to the ill person. The belief system is an empirical reality, and the patient's relationship to God in these dire circumstances is as much a part of the patient's being as his or her biochemistry is. In fact, those beliefs may affect that biochemistry favorably or unfavorably.

Fourth, however, there is a strong ethical content to the psychodynamic descriptions we have studied. From this angle of vision, the ethical contribution of psychological work to a theological and biblical understanding of temptation is a bridge between them. Ethical considerations from biblical theology can also contribute to the psychological understanding of inner conflict, just as surely as Shakespeare's insights inform both psychological and biblical interpretation.

For this to happen, however, both biblical theologians and psychologists need to be bilingual in both idioms, free of turf battlings, and with ears attuned to hear what Wordsworth called "the still, sad music of humanity." Humanity is a common concern, humanity in all its tornness.

6

Overcoming Temptation

Guidelines for identifying and understanding temptation and alternatives for overcoming them have been proposed throughout the book. They are intimately interwoven. Each chapter has described specific instances. The forms of temptation—the enticement of undisciplined desire, excuse-making, spiritual testing, the choice of a low aim for life, and the sleeping inattention of not watching—are exemplified by each new temptation that is mentioned. For example, take the temptation to despair that can at times be a prelude to suicide. Despair is an enticement to end the pain. The person is being enticed to end the pain of testing by killing himself or herself. Then, who knows, perhaps his or her rage at a specific person goes so far that suicide or a suicide attempt is a last-ditch effort to control the person at whom they are angry. However, in this chapter we will devote our primary attention to the day-to-day battle of conscience with temptation.

The Responsible Self

The human condition is plagued by several generic temptations. As the Lord God said to Cain, "Sin is couching at the door; its desire is for you, but you must master it" (Gen. 4:7). The metaphor of the door implies the same truth as in the Spirit of Christ's words to the Church at Laodicea in Revelation 3:20: "Behold, I stand at the door and knock; if any one hears my voice and opens the door, I will come in to him and eat with him, and he with me." The metaphor implies a strong central self in which each of us controls whom we will "let in."

Heinz Kohut (pp. 49, 35) speaks of the "nuclear self," which he has "conceptualized as an independent autonomous unit." He calls it "that specific self," which is the carrier of two conditions: (1) The nuclear self is the carrier of our grandiosity, the trait that embodies what I call in chapter 2 the "subtlest temptation," the temptation to play God, to replace God, to be God. (2) The nuclear self also embodies ideals and "sets its sights on values and ideals which are the descendants of the idealized parent ego."

I would add to Kohut's description of these ideals as being from the parents. Certainly that is true, but parents are not the only or even the most pervasive source of ideals. Teachers and especially the late-adolescent peer group are also sources of these ideals, as the young person individuates from his or her parents. In addition, the person responds both to the parents and to the adolescent peer group and teachers in the formation of his or her ideals, or lack of them.

This autonomous self decides to "let in" either the sin that couches at the door or the Spirit of Christ standing at the door and knocking. Rather than call this self just the nuclear self or the autonomous self, I prefer to call it what Richard Niebuhr does, the *responsible* self, in his book by this title. The purpose of prayer, he writes (p. 48), is to know ourselves and to seek guidance from God "as we decide, choose, commit ourselves, and otherwise bear the burden of our necessary human freedom."

To this self is presented the basic or generic temptations inherent in our human condition. The force that we "let in" determines the kind of person we become. Our nuclear self can either become the embodiment of evil (the devil, or Satan) or the Christ formed in us, as the apostle Paul says to the Galatians. ("My little children, with whom I am again in travail until Christ be formed in you!"—Gal. 4:19.) Thus the struggle with temptation is essentially the process of character formation.

The struggle of character formation is another way of saying what temptation is. The objective of the personal Christian life is that Christ be formed in us, that the indwelling Christ be our mighty fortress against letting in the forces of evil and becoming the incarnation of the Evil One. In this struggle, basic temptations inherent in all of us at all times become evident.

The responsible self has a master, comprehensive makeup and formation that resolves and wards off temptation without great effort or much internal conflict. The most comprehensive antidotes to temptation are a clear sense of personal integrity and a strong sense of mission. Such persons cannot be deterred by trivial pursuits. They know who they are under God, and they consider the temptations that beset many other persons to be alien—a sort of "not me." They have a life-encompassing cause to which they have committed themselves. Anything which deters them from that mission is pushed aside by the power of that mission. This integrity and this mission make of them a responsible self with a good immune system to a wide range of temptation.

Even so, such persons have a code, a set of convictions, and a profound insight into and honesty with themselves that deals with the ever-present temptations common to our humanity. By the very reason of being human, we are constantly presented with temptations that may even appear as shining examples for people around to praise us. A few of these follow.

Facing Up to Arrogance

As stated in chapter 2, the subtlest of temptations is to act as if we are God, to play God, or to exercise the fantasy of total control over ourselves and others. We could state this temptation in a more self-respecting manner by saying that we are seeking to become humble, the antithesis of arrogance. However, even humility, sought as an end in itself, becomes a subtle form of competition with others to be more humble than they are, a glazed-over form of arrogance. Humility seems to be more a by-product of our battle with arrogance than an end in itself.

Therefore, overcoming arrogance is to call it what it is—arrogance, taking too much upon oneself as one's right, and making unwarrantable claims as to one's own importance. To quote Charles Darwin, "The arrogant man looks down on others, and with lowered eyelids hardly condescends to see them" (*Oxford English Dictionary* I. 463).

An intentional daily self-examination for manifestations of arrogance anticipates and nips in the bud our yielding to many other temptations that disguise themselves as arrogance. This is no easy task; as Fr. Lorenzo Scupoli, in meditations written in 1589 entitled *Spiritual Combat,* says (Barns translation, p. 105): "Having entered into the snare of pride, they make an idol of their own understanding." To combat this he suggests "mental prayer," by which he means lifting up the mind to God with an "actual or virtual request for what is desired." Actual prayer happens when actual words are uttered and grace is asked for. In this instance, it would be a prayer for the grace of God to free us from arrogance. Virtual prayer is when "the mind is lifted up to obtain some grace showing Him our need without . . . words or reasons." He says, "Humbly and faithfully waiting for His help, I gaze and gaze upon the Lord" (pp.

229–230). Or, as the apostle Paul says, "And we all, with unveiled face, beholding the glory of the Lord, are being changed into his likeness from one degree of glory to another" (2 Cor. 3:18). Thus we move from temptation to transformation.

Lust for Power and Sex

Usually we think of lust as a purely sexual temptation. Rather, it is a compound temptation composed of the lust for power as well as the lust for sex. Jesus speaks of lusting in one's heart as adultery. He uses the surgical metaphor of cutting off a hand or plucking out an eye in Matthew 5:27–30. However, he uses the same figure of speech again in Matthew 18:27–29 in referring to the disciples' competitive power drives to know who was greatest in the kingdom of heaven. Then again, the apostle Paul speaks of the power factor in the sexual relationship between husbands and wives. "For the wife does not rule [or have power] over her own body, but the husband does; likewise the husband does not rule [or have power] over his own body, but the wife does" (1 Cor. 7:4). In this power-laden relationship, separation from each other over long periods of time and refusal of sexual relationships on either person's part gives Satan an opportunity to "tempt you through lack of self-control." (v. 5).

This temptation has already been discussed; but the addition here is the power-sex connection in the marital relationship. Instead of "Who is the greatest in the kingdom of heaven?" the question becomes "Who is going to tell the other what he or she can or can't or should or must do?" Slipping into this mode of competitive power seeking, marital partners are likely to use sexual relationships as weapons in the struggle for power.

In counseling with people who are living together without marriage, one finds the struggle for power is much the same. Sometimes the issue of power collects around the division of labor in doing the chores that maintain a home, sometimes power centers around financial management, sometimes it revolves about specifically sexual behavior. At other times it is a mixture of all three. Not being married does not remove this power struggle. It may even intensify it.

Resisting and conquering this temptation to an amalgam of sex and power calls for the cultivation of deliberate and well-thought-out considerateness of each other. First Peter 3:7 exhorts husbands to "live considerately with your wives [as] joint heirs of the grace of life, in order that your prayers may not be hindered." The King James translation is more literal, "according to knowledge," which means to understand in terms of the revelation of God in Christ and God's creation of us. The same thing could be said to women, who are to be exhorted to dwell considerately—or according to knowledge—with their husbands. A woman is to be known as being made in God's image and as a fellow participant in the grace of life. She has a specific kind of knowledge in the sexual union. She is to be trusted with knowledge and considerateness, not treated in ignorance, insensitivity, and without regard to her participation with her husband in the knowledge of God they have seen in the face of Jesus Christ.

Resisting temptation in the power-sex sphere calls for intense discernment and self-examination as to the direction from which the temptation is coming. It is easy to deceive ourselves by deleting the subtle power motive. "Who's in charge here and has the right to do as he or she pleases while everyone else in the family fits in as best they can?"

Nevertheless, the temptation to be involved in illicit or promiscuous sex presents itself in many ways without much reference to the power motive, and so does the power motive apart from the sexual motive. One of Gerald May's patients described dealing with his sexual fantasies: "I don't fight the fantasy off; I don't try to put it out of my mind, I just don't indulge in it, and it goes away. . . . It's like getting rid of an alley cat. You don't have to kick it; just don't feed it" (*Addiction and Grace*, p. 159).

With these as metaphors, let me suggest that we cannot prevent the sexual enticements that are all around us daily. They present themselves to both sexes. Homosexual persons have the same pressures upon them. However, we can challenge the temptation while it is still a temptation, before it becomes a calculated plan and we have decided to act upon our temptation. B. F. Skinner makes this clear when he says, "Deciding is not the execution of an act but the preliminary behavior responsible for it" (*Science and Human Behavior*, p. 243). In other words, deciding is premonitory or preamble behavior.

At this preliminary stage, through the infusion of the wisdom of God and the exercise of our own discernment and discretion, we can put a stop to "making a plan of action." That is where sexual attraction becomes lust—when we begin to devise plans of action, the preliminary behavior responsible for licentiousness.

However, if a person is gripped by a blind, compulsive, and driven kind of sexual behavior of whatever kind, this person needs a confessor or spiritual director to explore the depths of the obsession and help intercede for the divine strength to deal with this entrenched habit at its roots. Furthermore, if the person can join a group of those with similar problems who have convenanted together in prayer to aid and comfort one another in their struggle to overcome their habit, this is a double fortification against the temptation. Often such habits are expressions of the anger, alienation, and loneliness of the person.

Furthermore, in such behavior, the faithful God we worship rarely provides a single, sudden end to the temptation for all time to come. More commonly, God provides a daily manna of surcease from the habit for the twenty-four hours the person is living in—sometimes only for an hour at a time. These fellowships of suffering, encompassing a wide range of problems other than sexual addiction, combine struggles to enable its members to conquer temptation.

Courage for the Testing of Growing Up

One of the most effective ways of resisting and overcoming temptation is to pay attention to the demands of growing up and martialing the courage to put away childish things. The opposite of this is to give in to the fear of change and shrink back from the claims of maturity.

One of the most common examples of temptation as testing is the life changes a person has to make in the process of growing up. These times of testing have been described as "developmental tasks." They are rites of passage, such as the bar mitzvah or confirmation represents, and provide community support for the young person moving into the measure of maturity that is adolescence. Marriage is also certainly a time of testing, for one's capacity for intimacy and tenderness. And retirement puts older persons to strenuous tests of their capacity to live life without work as an assurance of their personal worth. Can they now live a life of grace?

Rarely are these developmental crises spoken of as "temptation" in a religious or moral sense. Nevertheless, a person is put to the test as to whether he or she will move forward into maturity, shrink back into regression, or stand still, becoming less and less functional from that day forward.

The Temptation to Despair

When the apostle Paul said (1 Cor. 10:13) that no temptation has overtaken us that is not common to all people, he was speaking of the troubles and burdens that harass us, beleaguer us, and defy solution. We work at these stresses and work some more, but they will not come right. Every time we do something that might help, the situation simply gets worse. These situations are endless "no-end" griefs. An example of this is a spouse or a parent trying to have a positive effect on a mate or child who is beset by self-defeating behaviors. The person may be full of dreams but not willing to work at mundane jobs for support while realizing those dreams. He or she may get involved in irresponsible sex that results in multiple pregnancies. He or she may be involved in the drug scene and do everything from begging to stealing, even from loved ones, in order to support this habit. Name any of the thousand ills the flesh is heir to, and you have a long catalog of stresses.

This same passage in Paul's writings, as has been said before, also says that God is faithful and will, with the temptation, provide a way of escape or make an end to the temptation. This promise resonates with our spoken and our unvoiced prayers in which we wonder, "How long, O Lord, how long?" And when—month after month and year after year—no end is in sight, we are tempted to despair.

Another situation that pushes people to despair is the presence of a disabling disorder that is not fatal. The person is likely to live a full life span, while having to "live with" the disability. Examples are the multiple sclerosis patient, the cord-injured quadriplegic, the massively burned and badly disfigured but recovered person, the young person who suffers a stroke as a result of a case of the shingles—the list is a long one. No cure for these disorders is in sight. The person goes through a death of the previous self. Restoration to something more than a despairing existence means the resurrection of a new self.

A much more subtle and surprising temptation to despair is the person who strives to do everything perfectly. An adolescent must make a 4.0 average; 3.8 produces total shame and pushes the person into despair. Or a parent reviewing his or her history of raising children does so with an intense perfection. As the parent gets older, he or she continues to ruminate over the mistakes or perceived mistakes that were made. By any standard of measurement, the children grew to maturity and turned out better than expected. Yet the parent is tempted to despair because he or she did not do everything perfectly.

The temptation to despair is our most lethal temptation. Dietrich Bonhoeffer puts it this way in *Temptation* (*Creation and Fall* and *Temptation*, p. 98): "This is the decisive fact in the temptations of the Christian, that he is abandoned by all men, abandoned by God himself. His heart shakes, and has fallen into complete darkness. He himself is nothing." The lethality of despair lies in its companion temptation of suicide. In many instances the temptation of suicide expresses the temptation of omnipotence, to be our own God and make that fateful decision to end our life. Especially is this true in the effects of suicide on those left behind.

The temptations to despair, then, are crucifixion temptations. An old self must spiritually die and a new self that is genuinely human must be born. Such genuinely human selves are forgiving of themselves and others. They accept their own helplessness; they do not have control over people's lives, only their own. They do not have the power to force their will on others. Nor do they have responsibility for other persons' mistakes. As John Bunyan says, "Every fat [vat] must stand upon his bottom." Disabled persons who live this new life also deal with their own helplessness creatively. In addition, they realize that their new self is more than, other than, and different from their disease, disorder, or disability.

But to yield to the temptation of despair is built on the fantasy that there really is another alternative to the symbolic death of the old self and birth of a new self. That alternative is the temptation to suicide, which is the temptation to take over from God, to bring an end to our own suffering. We assume that our suffering is never going to end; we must take matters into our own hands in isolation from those who love us and in estrangement from God's providence when he said that he would make an end or provide a way of escape. Once again, as Scupoli says, such persons will "make an idol of their own understanding."

The temptation to kill oneself was very different for Moses, as it is for persons today who live life with a persistent sense of being responsible to God. Moses fell into despair trying to lead the children of Israel, who exasperated, exhausted, and infuriated both him and God. Moses went to pray to God.

> Wherefore hast thou afflicted thy servant? and wherefore have I not found favour in thy sight, that thou layest the burden of all this people upon me? Have I conceived all this people? have I begotten them, that thou shouldst say unto me, Carry them in thy bosom, as a nursing father beareth the sucking child, unto the land which thou swarest unto their fathers? (Num. 11:11–12, KJV).

Many suicidal persons today have deep anger and feelings of injustice toward God and people whom they know. However, Moses expressed his outrage directly to God in prayer.

The psalms likewise express the whole range of emotion in prayer (see Psalm 109). Of the many good fruits of pietistic Christianity, one is destructive: that our prayers have to be only of those "nice" Goody Two-Shoes feelings we have. The Bible and biblical characters were not so. They told it to God like it was. We only isolate ourselves from God by not opening our most negative feelings to God.

Moses is a good example for those of us who are tempted in our isolation and loneliness. Moses continues: "I am not able to bear all this people alone, because it is too heavy for me." He confesses his limitations and the loneliness of the load of responsibility. Then he does not tell God he is ready to die. He asks God to kill him: "And if thou deal thus with me, kill me, I pray thee, out of hand, if I have found favor in thy sight; and let me not see my wretchedness" (Num. 11:14–15, KJV).

Even in his total despair, Moses put the matter of his death into the hands of God, and God answered him! He asked Moses to gather seventy men of the elders of Israel and then took part of the load from Moses' shoulders and put it onto each of their shoulders. He created a community of suffering. Moses need no longer bear his burden alone.

Moses' story is both an admonition and a promise: admonition that in our times of temptation to despair we can reveal our darkest thoughts to God and God will not cast us out; promise that God will lead us out of our isolation to a community of care and into a fellowship of other burden bearers. God's admonition and promise make life worth living and heal us of our suicidal thoughts.

Therefore, when we are tempted to despair, let us pour out our complaints before the Lord as did Moses and Hannah (1 Sam. 1:12–17) and ask God's guidance to a fellowship of other people who will share our responsibilities with us.

The Stewardship of Temptation

Temptation is a time of decision and destiny. We shape our own destinies by the decisions we make. Temptation presents us with alternative paths of action. The most basic set of alternatives is the kind of god or God we choose to serve. As Martin Luther says, "Temptation teaches us the true use and meaning of the first commandment, which none without afflictions and temptations shall rightly know or understand" (*Commentary on the Psalms*, p. 217). We have also seen how Gerald May relates our addictions to idolatry, the violation of the first commandment.

A second set of alternatives in time of temptation appears when we dare to take the time to gather facts and contemplate the consequences of the different and warring impulses to which we are prone to respond. In a third set of alternatives, God in Christ has not left us in isolation either. One of the gifts of the Holy Spirit is to be able to discern between spirits. We can pray for "the strong meat" of the Gospel designed for mature adults, as Hebrews 5:14 says.

When in a given tempting stress you decide to "say no," you forfeit that which is obviously evil for you and all those for whom you are responsible. Yet much creative but undisciplined good inheres in the direction we reject; there is much that is creative and good, yet it is "runaway" good, good that is without spiritual direction. Its strength is unbridled, unharnessed, and undisciplined. Is this creativity to be allowed to continue to run amok, causing trouble rather than edifying the sphere of relationships in which it moves?

Martin Buber says no, emphatically no! In *Images of Good and Evil* (p. 42) he quotes Psalm 86:11, "Unite my heart to fear thy name," and describes "the evil urge" as

> passion, that is, the power peculiar to man, without which he cannot beget or bring forth, but which, left to itself, remains without direction and leads astray, and the "good urge" is pure direction, in other words, as an unconditional direction, that toward God. To unite the two urges implies: to equip the absolute potency of passion with the one direction that renders it capable of great love and of great services. Thus and not otherwise can man be made whole.

In psychoanalytic terms this is the sublimation of unacceptable impulses and drives by diverting them into personally and socially acceptable channels. In theological terms it is the union of impulse and direction in the pure worship of God and the genuine care of those people a person is tempted to use, hurt, or exploit for his or her own purposes. Through this stewardship of temptation we are led into a higher and longer-lasting satisfaction and into the edification rather than the exploitation of our neighbor.

Jesus' Final Words on Temptation

Jesus himself went through the wilderness temptations and was tested by most of the scribes and Pharisees on every hand. He was tempted again in the garden of Gethsemane to invalidate the decision he had made in the wilderness by negating the destiny of the cross. He resisted and was speaking from the pressure of that temptation when he said, "The spirit indeed is willing, but the flesh is weak" (Mark 14:38). If he had chosen the flesh, he would have capitulated to the Pharisees, conformed to their system, possibly worked his way up to be a rabbi in a synagogue or an officer in the Sanhedrin superstructure. He might have married and fathered children, because that was the order of the day for Jewish men and women. The Jewish community, which had been nearly wiped out several times, needed children, especially sons. All of this is conjecture, but it is based on what we know of the culture of Jesus' day. The whole purpose of this fleshly existence rested in the lively hope that the Messiah would come in mighty political and military power and vanquish the Roman oppressor. Had not Cyrus done just that when they were captives in Babylon? The Lord speaks to Cyrus, his "anointed" (Isa. 45:1), and says of him, "He is my shepherd, and shall perform all my pleasure: even saying to Jerusalem, Thou shalt be built; and to the temple, Thy foundation shall be laid" (Isa. 44:28, KJV).

But Jesus had chosen the way of the spirit, with the longer vision that reached beyond the temple, Jerusalem, and the synagogue—even beyond the stinging power of death unto the resurrection and a kingdom that is not made with hands.

Consequently, by example and then by word, Jesus gave three last imperatives about handling temptation: watch, pray, and read the scriptures. (Jesus set the example for us by using the scriptures to deal with temptation.)

Watch

Jesus told his disciples to watch. He had sent them forth as sheep among wolves. They were to be wise as serpents and harmless as doves. To him there was no substitute for an intelligence consecrated to God. They had ears. They were to use them. They had eyes. They were to use them. They were to watch the ecclesiastical-political games the high priest and his coterie played with one another and with the Romans. They were to sustain a peaceful detachment from them. They were to care for the hungry, the thirsty, the stranger, the naked, the sick, and those in prison. They were anointed to preach good news to the poor, to proclaim the recovering of sight to the blind, to set at liberty those who were oppressed, to proclaim the acceptable year of the Lord. This was and is the way of the Spirit. They were at the risk of crucifixion.

If they accomplished this mission they would have to be constantly on the alert if they were to survive. Jesus admonishes us to exert this same watchful discernment and vocation, lest we enter into temptation. This concern fills the house swept clean of evil spirits and leaves no room for seven more to take their place.

Pray

Jesus' second admonition is that we pray. Prayer forces attention upon God and away from our desires. As Gerald May says, "For me, the energy of our basic desire for God is the human spirit, planted within us and nourished endlessly by the Holy Spirit of God" (*Addiction and Grace,* p. 92). This centering of our desires upon God dislodges and decentralizes attachments, fixations, and compulsions to and toward the addictions that beset us.

Prayer, furthermore, becomes a thinking upward way of life. It consists of repeatedly asking for God's perspective on the tempting forces at hand. Thus we are not alone in a mere dialogue between contending forces shut up in our own mind. We are in a trialogue in which God in the Holy Spirit is our teacher, bringing back to our memory all the things Jesus has taught us.

Read the Scriptures

The Holy Spirit does not bring to our remembrance something that was never there in the first place. Jesus facing his temptations in the wilderness was equipped with a thorough knowledge of Old Testament scripture. He overcame each of the devil's deceptive temptations by the strength of his remembered knowledge of the word of God. The language and thought of the Bible is not as well known today. But Jesus answers us that in the testing and tempting stresses we face, it is given to us by the Holy Spirit what to say—which is a form of action, a doing of the will of God. The *Book of Common Prayer* has us pray to God that "we may read, mark, learn, and inwardly digest" the scriptures. According to Jesus' example, this is a mighty fortification in times of temptation.

But What Kind of God?

It is easy enough to assume that others have the same perception of God that we have. But counselees often present gods that are foreign to the Jesus of the four Gospels. They present magical conceptions of God, tyrannical monsters as their god, or they have written off the whole pursuit of a habitual vision of the greatness of God. Most of these foreign conceptions of God are remnants of teachings they received when very young. We all tend to move developmentally, from experiencing God as an enemy, to thinking of God as a void of empty meaning-lessness, to the discovery of God as our friend. The clearest revelation we can find of that Friend is the Jesus Christ of the four Gospels. He is no God of the confusion of temptation, but of the peace of the single-minded, undivided loyalty of us to him and him to us. The God we speak of in this test is the God and Father of our Lord Jesus Christ, the Father of mercies and the God of all comfort. As Martin Luther says, "For it is not only perilous, but horrible to think of God without Jesus Christ" (*Commentary on the Psalms,* p. 319).

When we practice the disciplines for facing, dealing with, and becoming a good steward of our times of testing, we can enter into what James 1:2 calls the joy of temptation: "Count it all joy . . . when you meet various trials [temptations], for you know that the testing of your faith produces steadfastness."

7

The Providence of God and Temptation

The loneliness of the person under temptation makes it all the more burdensome. The very act of sharing with someone who is faithful and steadfast helps to ward off precipitous acts growing out of temptation. The good news of the Gospel is that Jesus Christ is our companion in the pressures of temptation. He has been there too. Furthermore, the eternal God is faithful, and the providence of God is at hand to clear a path through the temptation for us. At each of life's major developmental stages, we are free to choose to ignore the demands of maturity, quit growing, or even regress to a more childish level. But the intention of God is that we partake of the solid food of the word of God. For "solid food is for the mature, for those who have their faculties trained by practice to distinguish good from evil" (Heb. 5:14). God is the provider of that solid food.

Following the paradigm of the different meanings of temptation, this chapter deals with God's testing of us through the developmental crises of life. God does this not as a punitive act but as a constant challenge to us to grow up by making the crucial ethical and spiritual choices of life. The story of Abraham offering up Isaac forms the biblical basis for illustrating the testing of our willingness to grow in our own maturity and in our knowledge of God.

One of the best-known passages on temptation in the New Testament is found in Paul's First Letter to the Corinthians. This is most often quoted incompletely and out of context to say only that God "will not let you be tempted beyond your strength." However, the whole context (1 Cor. 10:12–14) is as follows:

> Therefore let any one who thinks that he [or she] stands take heed lest he [or she] fall. No temptation has overtaken you that is not common to man. God is faithful, and he will not let you be tempted beyond your strength, but with the temptation will also

provide the way of escape [or, make an end], that you may be able
to endure it. Therefore, my beloved, shun the worship of idols.

The context of this passage is that the Corinthians were par-
ticipating in pagan worship. They took food during that worship, along with their pagan friends. Paul understands how
easy it was for them to fall into this practice. The slippery slope
of temptation is such that everybody must take heed lest they
slide into the worship of pagan idols. The temptation to revert
to idolatry was strong. They had to be doubly watchful. After
his assurance of God's faithfulness in helping them to bear the
temptation, he admonished them to shun the worship of idols.

Their friends still worshiping idols were the incarnation of
temptation to them. Yet Paul reminds them that they have a
friend in God who is faithful and not fickle, who is present in
strength with them in their hour of temptation. The key word
in this provocative passage is "provide." "God is faithful, and
he will not let you be tempted beyond your strength, but . . .
will also provide the way of escape, that you may be able to
endure it."

The word "provide" in the Greek is *poiēsei,* written in the
future active tense. An action word, it means "to do, to make,
manufacture, or produce." It refers to God's creative activity
as our Creator still at work at the very center of our temptations. God's providence, then, is historically related to God the
Creator having made us. He continues to create in the present.
Temptation is the arena of his creative work in us. He works in
us both to will and do his good pleasure. At the same time, God
sees ahead and provides or creates an end to the temptation.
Contemporary research on stress and stress management tells
us that a given stressor is far more easily borne if we know that
there is an *end* to it.

The passages of our lives from one stage of maturity to another present us with the temptation to choose a low aim for
the rest of our lives. If we mature, we take a leap of faith into
the unknown. Or, if we choose a low aim for our life, we shrink
back into the false security of the illusion that our lives as they
are at this moment are the best they will ever be. Thus we fixate
at the present stage of maturity. We may, under the pressure of
a passage such as taking our first job or retiring, regress to an
earlier time when we were free of the burdens of responsible,
mature living. God, working through God's own creation,
made us to grow and mature. In this sense we are tested by
God as Creator at each developmental crisis of our lives. We
are called by God as Redeemer in Jesus Christ out of our low

aims for our existence into the high callings that Jesus the Christ has for us.

The Creator, Providence, and Creativity

The passage from First Corinthians calls into action three dimensions of what is going on when we are being tempted: God as Creator, God as provider, and God stimulating creativity in us to bring an end to our bondage to idolatry. He opens the way to new life in Christ.

In popular thinking, people tend to think of God the Creator as having created the world in a moment of time and left it with us to manage. I prefer to think of God as does John Macquarrie, in *Principles of Christian Theology* (p. 219):

> No sharp distinction can be made between creation and providence, for we did not tie creation to a moment of time at the beginning, but interpreted the doctrine of creation as meaning the dependence of the beings at all times on Being that lets them be. . . . The assertion of God's providence is just another way of asserting his constant creating and sustaining energy.

Macquarrie goes further and says that belief in providence cannot effectively be grounded in metaphysical logic but is most often found existentially in the course of events.

> It is through happenings that increase and strengthen our being— that do so not because of our own efforts primarily, but sometimes in spite of our own efforts—that we come to a belief in providence; and we do so because in these happenings we have become aware of the presence of Being, acting on us and in us, and giving itself to us (p. 220).

He cites examples of this in the exodus from Egypt and the cross and resurrection of Jesus Christ through which God created communities of faith who look upon these events as evidence of the providence of God. He says that "perhaps the clearest and earliest statement of a belief in providence occurs in the story of Joseph. . . . Joseph's story points to events which *in spite of* the intention of human agents have turned out for good" (p. 221). Conviction as to the providence of God is gestated and born in us when we experience his deliverance from temptation, disaster, or even certain death. This deliverance is branded on our memory and remembered at later times of temptation or threat of destruction.

Belief in the reality of providence seems to be rooted in an individual or group experience of deliverance after the fact. Assurance of God's providence in an ongoing situation is the basis of endurance of the "times of testing," the times of temptation. The central meaning of Paul's statement in 1 Cor. 10:12–14 is that God is at work in the eye of the storm of temptation, creating a new and better person or community. God's creation continues, to use Fritz Kunkel's title for his exegesis of the book of Matthew *(Creation Continues)*. To put it graphically, God *rested* on the seventh day, but after that, and until your and my last temptation, God is at work creating a new being of us in Jesus Christ and in regenerating the community of faith made up of us and our fellow strugglers with temptation.

A Biblical Case History

The moving story of Abraham, Sarah, and Isaac demonstrates the dynamic relationship between God's providence and Abraham's being tested or tempted in much the way Paul describes the providence and presence of God with us as providing a way of escape during severe times of temptation. It also illustrates the creative growth of Abraham's spirituality as he went through the ordeal.

Isaac was the only child of Abraham and Sarah, born to them in their advanced years, as is dramatized in the visitation of the three messengers of God who came to them and told them they would have a child. "Sarah laughed to herself, saying, 'After I have grown old, and my husband is old, shall I have pleasure?' " (Gen. 18:12). And the Lord wondered with Abraham why Sarah laughed. When Abraham raised the question with Sarah she denied it for she was afraid, but Abraham said, "No, but you did laugh" (Gen. 18:15). "The LORD visited Sarah [and] did to Sarah as he had promised. And Sarah conceived, and bore Abraham a son in his old age at the time of which God had spoken to him" (Gen. 21:1–2). They named him Isaac. "And Sarah said, 'God has made laughter for me; every one who hears will laugh over me. . . . Who would have said to Abraham that Sarah would suckle children? Yet I have borne him a son in his old age' " (Gen. 21:6–7).

The testing and temptations of Abraham and Sarah during the long years of their infertility had come to an end. The providence of God had "made an end" to their testing. They had escaped the stress of childlessness. But hardly had one stress been relieved before an even more subtle temptation began to grow.

You can imagine how much this one son meant to Abraham

and Sarah. You can readily see how Isaac would come to mean *too much* to them for their or his own good. Could it be that they idolized him? We can only surmise that they worshiped the ground Isaac walked on. They were once again in the crucible of temptation. The idolatry of children is one of the most socially approved idolatries, then and now. Parental overpossessiveness and overprotectiveness denies the child the right to make his or her own mistakes. It substitutes the parent's judgment for the child's instead of developing the child's own capacity to make and put into action wise and mature decisions. Therefore, the idolatry of the child is followed by the sacrifice of the child when years have passed and the parents no longer have any control over the child's thinking and actions.

If this does not happen routinely in the second decade of the child's life, it may happen traumatically when both parents have died. Thus they leave the child with the legacy of an undeveloped moral judgment and a retarded sense of personal responsibility for his or her own acts. Once again God enters the center stage of their temptation to test them. It is wise to say "them" advisedly, because the story in Genesis 22 does not refer to Sarah at all. Women of her day were vocal and direct with their opinions and had power in the family and beyond the family. But Sarah stayed at home and is silent in the written account of Genesis 22. Only Abraham perceives the Lord requiring him to offer up Isaac as a burnt offering. We are left to wonder what Sarah thought of this.

Gerhard von Rad calls this the "great temptation" of Abraham. The story reveals a very important meaning and function of temptation in the creative growth both of Abraham and of persons like you and me. Temptation into which God calls us is qualitatively different from any other kind of temptation, such as that arising from our own lusts and desires. The temptation into which God pushes us is a life-and-death teaching experience in which his grace and providential care become unforgettably real to us. God's testing comes in God's call to a higher maturity. Providence thus learned is not only held intellectually, as it is when we learn from a book or from a logical metaphysical speculation. Providence learned this way is unforgettable. God teaches us in such a way that we cannot forget. Logical metaphysics teaches us in such a way that we have to memorize it for a test and keep the book in which it is written to remind us later. From this text God is the Teacher, the student is given a laboratory exam, and the teaching objective is that the student shall learn viscerally the providence of God in the crucible of temptation.

God tested Abraham. He said, "Abraham!" Abraham replied, "Here am I." They were present to each other, and Abraham knew he was in the presence of God. Then God commanded Abraham: "Take your son, your only son Isaac, whom you love, and go to the land of Moriah, and offer him there as a burnt offering upon one of the mountains of which I shall tell you" (Gen. 22:2).

From this scene you and I can observe that God made special mention to Abraham that Isaac was his *only* son and that Abraham loved him. Is there any possibility that God was in essence challenging Abraham's idolizing Isaac and Abraham was being put to the test as to who God is? We can only speculate. Suffice it to say that Abraham obeyed the Lord's commands and did as he was told. Of this we can be sure: Abraham's obedience was being tested. Abraham cut the wood for a burnt offering, saddled his ass, and took two of his servants and his son Isaac with him. They found the mountain, and, leaving the two servants, Abraham went up the mountain with Isaac, who was now bearing the wood for the burnt offering. Abraham took the fire and the knife.

Isaac asked his father, "Where is the lamb for a burnt offering?" Here Abraham expressed his faith in the providence of God. God had brought him through many trials, and he was counting on his providence again. He said, "God will provide himself the lamb for a burnt offering, my son" (Gen. 22:8).

They proceeded to the climactic moment when Abraham raised the knife to kill his son. But the angel of the Lord said, "Do not lay your hand on the lad or do anything to him; for now I know that you fear God, seeing you have not withheld your son, your only son, from me" (Gen. 22:12). Abraham discovered a ram caught in the thicket behind him and offered him up instead of Isaac. And he "called the name of that place The Lord will provide; as it is said to this day, 'On the mount of the Lord it shall be provided' " (Gen. 22:14).

The test was not only of God's providence in the grim encounter of Abraham with God. It was also a test of Abraham's obedience to God as he placed the worship of God above the love he had for his son. Notice that God mentions twice in his conversations with Abraham that Isaac was Abraham's *only* son. Abraham's possible idolatry of Isaac had been put to the test and God had made an end to his idolatry. Now, as the renewal of God's covenant with Abraham that follows this account indicates, Abraham and his *only* son (mentioned by God a third time) would multiply and the people of their descendants would be the instruments of God's blessings: "By your descendants shall all the nations of the earth bless themselves, because you have obeyed my voice" (Gen. 22:18).

Abraham had endured the temptation, and God had provided an escape and made an end to the temptation. God learned that Abraham was obedient to him and not an idolator of his only son. Abraham learned that God did indeed provide when he was obedient. Now the three of them could get on with the creation of the people of God, who would be a blessing to all nations. From that point forward the practice of substituting an animal for child sacrifice was legitimized until the situation was reversed and God's *only* Son, Jesus Christ, the Lamb of God that takes away the sin of the world, actually was sacrificed on the cross, but was buried and raised again on the third day. The laws against child sacrifice in Leviticus 20:1–5 and Deuteronomy 12:31 seem to indicate that among the earliest Hebrews child sacrifice may have been a practice. God continues in Jesus to provide for us and creatively instruct us in times when temptations to disobey his calling beset us. It was Jesus who said to us, "Truly, I say to you, there is no one who has left house or brother or sisters or mother or father or children or lands, for my sake and for the gospel, who will not receive a hundredfold now in this time, houses and brothers and sisters and mothers and children and lands, with persecutions, and in the age to come eternal life" (Mark 10:29–30).

This was and is one of the most radical expectations and promises of Jesus. He went against the tide of Jewish tradition, which saw the family as the ultimate value to be sustained. And, by extension, the Jewish nation was most favored and destined by God. Even today in Christian communities, primary obedience and loyalty to kinspersons makes for all sorts of family dysfunction, whereas primary obedience to the eternal God and devotion to the larger family of humankind are nebulous abstractions to us as idolators of parents, spouses, children, and family possessions.

However, that melancholy prophet of an atheistic view of the world, Sigmund Freud, said in this positive regard for the spiritual education of us all:

> "Apart from . . . pathological phenomena it may be said that in the present case religion achieved all the aims for the sake for which it is included in the education of the individual. It put a restraint upon his sexual tendencies by affording them a sublimation and safe mooring; it lowered the importance of his family relationships by giving him access to the great community of mankind" ("History of an Infantile Neurosis," pp. 114–115).

Through Abraham's trials the importance to him of his immediate family was lessened. He was given access to the greater community of all nations. He was released from a stifling bondage of idolatry to a liberated access to the larger family of humankind. This liberation came about through the heated crucible of Abraham's temptation—the great temptation.

Providence and Temptation in Jesus' Life

Jesus' temptations in the wilderness bear a remarkable resemblance to the ordeal of Abraham. Whereas the Lord himself went with Abraham through his temptation and at critical moments provided for him, Jesus was "led by the Holy Spirit for forty days in the wilderness, tempted by the devil." We do not find the devil incarnated in some earthly creature such as a serpent or in the person of, let us say, Simon Peter or Judas. Jesus confronts the devil *as such,* the father of lies that he later told his opponents the devil is. Yet, in both the Matthew 4 and Luke 4 accounts, the Father and the Holy Spirit are present, providing for the Son in an altogether new way. They appear in the lively word of the law of God. Each proposition of the devil is parried by Jesus with a specific quotation from scripture.

To the temptation to turn stones into bread, Jesus responds with Deuteronomy 8:3, a passage that reminds readers that God had humbled the people of God and let them hunger in the wilderness and fed them with manna in order to teach them that "man does not live by bread alone, but . . . by everything that proceeds out of the mouth of the LORD."

To the temptation to rule all the kingdoms of the world, Jesus answers with the meaty meaning of Deuteronomy 6:10–15 and a specific quotation of Deuteronomy 6:13. The passage reminds readers that the people of God were delivered up out of the land of Egypt by the might and power of the Lord. They were provided for by him, and they were to have no other gods but him to worship.

To the temptation to cast himself down from the temple, the devil caught on to the skill of Jesus and the Lord's providential care of him through the power of the Torah with which Jesus answered him. The devil leads off with a passage of his own choosing, Psalm 91:11–12. Once again Jesus responds with Deuteronomy 6, this time verse 16: "You shall not put the LORD your God to the test." As Shakespeare said in *The Merchant of Venice* (I.iii.99), "The devil can cite Scripture for his purpose."

These three utterances of Jesus from the Torah remind us of his teaching his disciples not to take thought of what to say when they are being put to the test in the courts because in that hour the Holy Spirit will give them the words. However, these three statements also point to the empirical reality that Jesus had learned the Torah through intensive study beforehand. The Holy Spirit enlivened his memory; he was provided with the word of God from the storehouse he had laid up in his obedience to God in the study of the Torah. The awesome way in which Jesus could answer the tempter and the host of critics who repeatedly put him to the test bespeaks both the massive memory he had from his study of the Word and the quickening power provided by the Holy Spirit in retrieving from his memory bank the precise scripture passage required for each occasion.

The incarnation of God in Jesus Christ was no partial or incomplete work. Jesus' brain was related to God the Father and God the Holy Spirit during his time on earth in the same confining and limiting way our brains are. As Hebrews 5:8 says, "Although he was a Son, he *learned* obedience through what he suffered" (emphasis added). When he was in the wilderness, he suffered the temptations of the devil. As Hebrews 4:15 puts it, "For we have not a high priest who is unable to sympathize with our weaknesses, but one who in every respect has been tempted as we are, yet without sin." He had laid up the Torah in his heart. When the pressure of temptation was on, the Holy Spirit brought back to him that which had been stored in his memory through disciplined study, that he might not sin against the Lord. In the word of God he experienced the providence of God. The scripture, therefore, is not something to be talked about or to be the object of worship and controversy. The scripture is to be read, marked, learned, and inwardly digested; it is to be laid up in the heart for times of temptation. With it we can take heed lest we fall into idolatry, even of the unread, unheeded scriptures themselves.

These passages bring a fresh light on Psalm 119:11: "I have laid up thy word in my heart, that I might not sin against thee." They reveal the function of the *learned* scriptures in our spiritual history, and for that matter in the spiritual history of a social grouping of people. No substitute exists for knowing what the Bible really does say. The Holy Spirit does not automatically insert the actual words of scripture into our minds. Many people believe this, but Jesus himself said to his disciples, referring to his teaching, "I have said all this to you to keep you from falling away. They will put you out of the synagogues; indeed, the hour is coming when whoever kills you will think he is offering service to God. . . . But I have said these things to you, that when their hour comes you may *remember* that I told you of them" (John 16:1–2, 4; emphasis added). Then, again, in John 14:25–26: "These things I have spoken to you, while I am still with you. But the Counselor, the Holy Spirit, whom the Father will send in my name, he will teach you all things, and *bring to your remembrance* all that I have said to you" (emphasis added). The Holy Spirit works in the disciplined memory of the person who has laid up the words of Jesus in his or her heart, so that in the hour of temptation he or she may not sin against God. When temptation is at its worst and the heat of pressure is upon us, when we are stressed out with the lure and desire of that which is to our own destruction, we have the gift of the Holy Spirit and the memory of what Jesus taught us to keep us from falling. No wonder Jude, the saint of persons who are in dire circumstances, could write the benediction of verse 24: "Now to him who is able to keep you from falling and to present you without blemish before the presence of his glory with rejoicing, to the only God, our Savior through Jesus Christ our Lord, be glory, majesty, dominion, and authority, before all time and now and for ever. Amen."

Jesus' Teaching Disciples How to Pray

No discussion of providence and temptation is complete without attention to the Lord's Prayer (Matt. 6:9–13). The petitions in the prayer embody a steadfast confidence in God for daily bread, for forgiveness of sin, and for the strength to forgive those who have sinned against us, that we will not be led into temptation or put to the test of persecution, and that we will be delivered from evil.

These petitions are all fervent appeals to God to provide for us. They stand on the assumption that we believe that God in his providence is *present* as we eat our daily bread, as we struggle with the need to forgive and be forgiven, as we feel the magnetic pull of the power of evil, tempting us, and pray anxiously for deliverance. There is a commitment on our part that God is intimately involved in the processes of life. God works in them and in our consciousness of God's power to overrule the circumstances of our lives so that we will not be pushed into situations that put us to the test, or tempt us to evil. Furthermore, if this actually does happen, as it often does, God is present to deliver us.

In this prayer, no resort to magic is asked. Full personal responsibility on our part is accepted for the disciplines of forgiving those who have sinned against us and for the strength to resist temptation at the same time that we ask for God's protection and assistance in the task. The mechanisms of defense—such as projection of responsibility onto others, pious reaction formations, the displacement of guilt onto circumstances, other objects, or persons, and so on—do not appear in this most inclusive and yet simplest statement of all prayers. An additional note needs to be made: The prayer is free of religious ideologies so that it includes all persons, of any faith group, who believe in God. It is a psychologically sound pattern of spiritual maturity and genuine humility for the thought life of an unbeliever. It is an antidote to the tendency to make oneself into God.

Jesus in the Garden of Gethsemane

Jesus' temptations in the wilderness reveal to us the work of the scriptures and of the Holy Spirit in the providence of God in his and our temptations. They reveal also the importance of our own memories as the stuff with which God's providence prepares us ahead of time for the hour of our temptation. In this sense, God's providence is a "seeing ahead" for us, a preparation and a buttressing against the forces of evil.

In Jesus' testing in the garden and his instruction to his sleepy-headed disciples, we find further fortification for our times of temptation. If we are emotionally overwhelmed by temptation, so was he. He was "greatly distressed and troubled." He said to his disciples, "My soul is very sorrowful, even to death" (Mark 14:33–34). The later addition to the Lucan account (Luke 22:43–44) says that he was "in an agony" and "prayed more earnestly; and his sweat became like great drops of blood falling down upon the ground." He was so distressed that a messenger of God (that is what an angel is!) visited him and strengthened him. This is reminiscent of Jesus' temptations in the wilderness, when messengers of God came and ministered unto him.

From both a theological and a psychological angle of vision, the Gospel writers themselves describe Jesus so vividly as to require little additional commentary as to what he was experiencing at this time. The human dimension of his person drew him to what his life might have been—to a wife and children, and, with his massive knowledge of the scripture, to being a power figure in the Sanhedrin. Yet in the divine dimension of his person, he had committed to the way of the cross. His prayer of commitment to the will of God settled the matter, but his memory of the struggle of affirming the will of God appeared in his witness to his disciples: "And he came to the disciples and found them sleeping; and he said to Peter, 'So, could you not watch with me one hour? Watch and pray that you may not enter into temptation; the spirit indeed is willing, but the flesh is weak' " (Matt. 26:40–41).

Temptation is the testing ground between the strivings of the image of God in us and the strivings of our desires to be the masters of our fate, the captains of our souls, between the callings of our spirits and the claims of our biological destinies as human beings. The latter claims are the sources of our addictions and idolatries. The former are the sources of our freedom and willingness to commend our spirits into the hands of God. To be given that freedom and willingness is the source of our serenity. We have, in Reinhold Niebuhr's words, the grace to accept with serenity the things in our world that cannot be changed, the courage to change the things that should be changed, and the wisdom to know the difference. In the crucible of temptation, we can appropriate the truth of Jesus' words: "The spirit indeed is willing, but the flesh is weak."

However, this is not all that Jesus said to Peter. He also said, as a preface to this remark, "Watch and pray that you may not enter into temptation." The wisdom of knowing the difference between the things we can and cannot change grows out of vigilantly watching the incomparable capacity of the human heart for self-deception and responsiveness to the threats of other people. Jesus knew the things that were happening to him now were in the future for his disciples. History bears out that he was right. So this admonition is like the one he gave them when he was sending them out as sheep among wolves, that they were to be wise as serpents and harmless as doves. Later, after the coming of the Holy Spirit, it would become the gift of discernment (1 Cor. 12:10), whereby the followers of Jesus would be able to distinguish between spirits—spirits of bondage and spirits of freedom, spirits of fear and spirits of love, spirits of rage and spirits of self-control, false prophets and true prophets. To exercise this gift they would have to stay awake and be watchful and pray that they themselves might not enter into temptation.

As we live life in the awareness of the providence of God in times of temptation, we gradually grow into an awareness of God as Creator. We discover the laws of health, the nourishment of spiritual and emotional maturity, and the ways in which ignorance or defiance of these laws leads to our own undoing. We are provided with hindsight in the assessment of the ways our own life history has bound us with unnecessary fears, legalisms, and taboos that erode our creativity. We are provided with insight into our own maladaptive actions, going against the calling of God to maturity, and see that they are no longer necessary. We develop foresight under the instruction of the Holy Spirit as to the meaning of the ethical teachings of Jesus. This foresight enables us to face the future with confidence and intelligence rather than with fear and ignorance. We grow into a creative serenity that sets us free to have new ideas, see new ways of serving our neighbor. We sense new ways of enhancing the beauty and livability of God's creation. We become co-laborers, co-creators, co-providers with God. We are no longer alone! This laboring together with God is the source of all creativity. This is God's providence at work in our behalf in the crucibles of our temptations.

Temptation and the Daily Providence of God

The presence and providence of God in our temptations—a persistent assumption throughout this chapter—is given to us on a here-and-now basis. It is not given to us to answer the anxieties, Luther's *Anfechtung* (see chapter 1), and the restless imaginations we have about the future. At the most basic level, the need for food, the source of Jesus' first temptation in the wilderness, the Lord provided manna one day at a time. Anything stored up for the future would on the second day be spoiled and not fit to eat. An exception was made for the sabbath, when a two-day supply was provided. The command of the Lord was: "Go out and gather a day's portion every day" (Ex. 16:4–5).

In the Lord's Prayer, the same spirit is maintained: "Give us this day our daily bread" (Matt. 6:11). At a higher, more psychological level than the need for bodily food, Jesus addresses the persistent temptation to overload ourselves with anticipatory anxiety about the future: "Therefore do not be anxious about tomorrow, for tomorrow will be anxious for itself. Let the day's own trouble be sufficient for the day" (Matt. 6:34).

I do not read this passage to mean that we are not to have foresight about building a house, for example, because one of Jesus' parables refers to a man who decided to build a house that he could not finish because he had not first sat down and counted the cost. Rather, I read the passage to mean that we are not to fret and fume about *what we imagine* the problems and troubles of tomorrow will be. Jesus addresses our temptation to live in constant dread and fear of the future.

Today we have a therapeutic revolution in the spontaneous formation of self-help groups. These groups support cancer patients, alcoholics, drug addicts, persons with chronic diseases like multiple sclerosis, manic depression, compulsive gambling, and many other such needy, isolating concerns of life. Uniformly, they deal with the temptations to addiction, despair, and rage that debilitating diseases such as, let us say, diabetes create. On a one-day-at-a-time basis they steadfastly encourage members to live life praying for strength to sustain themselves for that one day only, sometimes just for an hour at a time. Their fellowship of suffering removes their isolation and provides them the resonating support of other sufferers. Their commitment of their own helplessness and the unmanageableness of their lives to the power of God as they have come to know God heals them of their grandiosity and self-sufficiency.

It seems that God is indeed the *I am that I am* who met Moses at the burning bush. In the midst of our most pressing temptations, the presence of God provides sustenance and direction. In fact, as a very young granddaughter of one of my good friends says, we are met by God's providence in our temptations "right in the middle of now."

Works Cited

Abingdon Dictionary of Living Religions. Keith Crim, Roger A. Bullard, and Larry D. Shinn, eds. Nashville: Abingdon Press, 1981.

Allport, Gordon W. *Personality: A Psychological Interpretation.* New York: Henry Holt & Co., 1937.

Bainton, Roland H. *Here I Stand: A Life of Martin Luther.* Nashville: Abingdon Cokesbury Press, 1950.

Berne, Eric. *Games People Play.* New York: Grove Press, 1964.

———. *Transactional Analysis in Psychotherapy.* New York: Grove Press, 1961.

Bonhoeffer, Dietrich. *Creation and Fall,* and *Temptation.* New York: Macmillan Co., 1965.

Book of Common Prayer. New York: Oxford University Press, 1928.

Boorstin, Daniel J. *The Discoverers: A History of Man's Search to Know His World and Himself.* New York: Random House, 1985.

Buber, Martin. *Images of Good and Evil.* London: Routledge & Kegan Paul, 1952.

Calvin, John. *Commentaries on the First Book of Moses Called Genesis,* vol. 1. Tr. John King. Grand Rapids: Wm. B. Eerdmans Publishing Co., 1948.

Coles, Robert. *Children of Crisis, Vol. 1: A Study of Courage and Fear.* Boston: Little, Brown & Co., 1967.

———. *Children of Crisis, Vol. 2: Migrants, Mountaineers, and Sharecroppers.* Boston: Little, Brown & Co., 1972.

———. *Children of Crisis, Vol. 3: The South Goes North.* Boston: Little, Brown & Co., 1972.

———. *Children of Crisis, Vol. 5: Privileged Ones.* Boston: Little, Brown & Co., 1980.

Freud, Sigmund. *The Standard Edition of [His] Complete Psychological Works,* vol. 17. Tr. J. Strachey et al. London: Hogarth Press, 1959.

Friedman, Edwin H. *Generation to Generation: Family Process in Church and Synagogue.* New York: Guilford Press, 1986.

Habel, Norman C. *The Book of Job, A Commentary.* Old Testament Library. Philadelphia: Westminster Press, 1985.

Hall, Douglas John. *Lighten Our Darkness: Toward an Indigenous Theology of the Cross.* Philadelphia: Westminster Press, 1976.

Havel, Vaclav. *Letters to Olga.* Tr. Paul Wilson. New York: Henry Holt, 1989.

———. *Temptation.* Tr. Marie Winn. New York: Grove Press, 1989.

Horney, Karen. *Our Inner Conflicts.* New York: W. W. Norton & Co., 1945.

Hovland, C. Warren. "*Anfechtung* in Luther's Exegesis," in Franklin Littell, ed., *Reformation Studies.* Richmond: John Knox Press, 1962.

James, William. *Talks to Teachers on Psychology and to Students on Some of Life's Ideals.* Reprint of 1899 work. New York: Dover Publications, 1962.

Kaplan, Harold I., and Benjamin J. Sadock. *Comprehensive Textbook of Psychiatry,* 4th ed. Baltimore: Williams & Wilkins Co., 1984.

Kennan, George F. *Sketches from a Life.* New York: Pantheon Books, 1989.

King, Martin Luther, Jr. *Stride Toward Freedom.* New York: Harper & Brothers, 1958.

Kohut, Heinz. *Self Psychology and the Humanities.* New York: W. W. Norton & Co., 1985.

Leehan, James. *Pastoral Care for Survivors of Family Abuse.* Philadelphia: Westminster Press, 1989.

Lifton, Robert. *The Broken Connection: On Death and the Continuity of Life.* New York: Simon & Schuster, 1979.

Luther, Martin. *Commentary on the Psalms.* London: W. Sunkin & R. Marshall, 1819.

———. *Luther's Large Catechism.* Tr. Robert H. Fischer. Philadelphia: Fortress Press, 1959.

Macquarrie, John. *Principles of Christian Theology.* New York: Charles Scribner's Sons, 1966.

Manson, T. W. *The Epistle to the Hebrews.* London: Hodder & Stoughton, 1951.

May, Gerald. *Addiction and Grace.* New York: Harper & Row, 1988.

McCrum, Robert, William Cran, and Robert MacNeil. *The Story of English.* New York: Viking Press, 1986.

Menninger, Karl. *Whatever Became of Sin?* New York: Hawthorn Books, 1973.

Niebuhr, H. Richard. *Responsible Self.* New York: Harper & Row, 1963.

Nietzsche, Friedrich. *Joyful Wisdom.* Tr. Thomas Common. New York: Frederick Ungar Publishing Co., 1960.

Oates, Wayne E., and Charles E. Oates, M.D. *People in Pain.* Philadelphia: Westminster Press, 1985.

Peck, M. Scott. *People of the Lie.* New York: Simon & Schuster, 1983.

Ropes, John H. *The International Critical Commentary on the Epistle of St. James.* Edinburgh: T. & T. Clark, 1954.

Scupoli, Lorenzo. *Spiritual Combat.* Tr. Thomas Barns. London: Methuen & Co., 1950.

Sheehan, William, and Jerome Kroll. "Psychiatric Patients' Belief in General Health Factors and Sin as Causes of Illness." *American Journal of Psychiatry* 147:1 (Jan. 1990).

Skinner, B. F. *Science and Human Behavior.* New York: Macmillan Co., 1953.

Spiegel, Leo. "Superego and the Function of Anticipation with Comments on

Anticipatory Anxiety." In *Psychoanalysis: A General Psychology,* ed. R. M. Lowenstein et al. New York: International Universities Press, 1966.

Tillich, Paul. *The Courage to Be.* New Haven, Conn.: Yale University Press, 1952.

————. *Systematic Theology,* vols. 1 and 2. Chicago: University of Chicago Press, 1951, 1957.

Westermann, Claus. *Genesis 37–50.* Minneapolis: Augsburg Publishing House, 1986.